Introductory Physical Science

EIGHTH EDITION

WITH FORMATIVE ASSESSMENT

Uri Haber-Schaim
Peter Gendel
H. Graden Kirksey
Harold A. Pratt

Science Curriculum Inc., Belmont, Massachusetts 02478

Introductory Physical Science
Eighth Edition

Uri Haber-Schaim, Peter Gendel, H. Graden Kirksey,
Harold A. Pratt

Credits
Editor: Sylvia Gelb
Book Design and Production:
    SYP Design & Production Inc.,
    www.sypdesign.com
Photography:
    Benoit Photography: pages 2, 13, 27, 50, 54, 59, 79, 89,
    91, 137, 138, 149, 173,177
    Douglas Christian: pages 3, 20, 49, 80, 117, 121
    Susan van Etten: pages 1, 4, 15, 17, 18, 19, 49, 67, 89, 95,
    101, 109, 134, 152, 153, 154, 156, 173
    Stevie Grand/Science Photo Library: page 131
    Jesse Adams: page 41
    Jan Sullivan/PDPhoto.org: page 149
Photo researcher: Susan van Etten
Graphics:
    Ashley van Etten: pages 10, 11, 196, 197, 200

Printed in the United States of America
By Quebecor World

ISBN 1-882057-25-2

10 9 8 7 6 5 4 3 2 1

Preface to the Eighth Edition

The Eighth Edition of *Introductory Physical Science* (*IPS*) provides a powerful adaptation of a fine-tuned program to meet the needs of a wide variety of schools. Without compromising the integrity, structure, or storyline of the course, we have streamlined the early chapters to allow students to reach the atomic model earlier in the school year. By replacing the three chapters on electric charge and ions with a new chapter on the periodic table, we have placed more emphasis on material that is required by many state frameworks.

A new component, included in both this text and the *Teacher's Guide and Resource Book*, is the many new formative assessment questions specially suited for a quick response by the entire class. Many studies have shown that the sensible utilization of formative assessment produces significant improvement in understanding and retention. In this text the formative assessment questions are color-coded to differentiate them from other section questions. Additional formative assessment questions appear in the *Teacher's Guide and Resource Book* for use orally by the teacher.

Acknowledgments

Many of the formative assessment questions were field-tested during the spring of 2003 and the fall of 2004. We are indebted to the following teachers for providing us with feedback:

Bruce Dudek, St. Labre Catholic Indian High School, Ashland, MT

Billy Fitzgerald, Isidore Newman School, New Orleans, LA

Peter Gendel, Isidore Newman School, New Orleans, LA

Denise LeBlond, Gilkey Middle School, Portland, OR

Jan Meyers, Bell Middle School, Golden, CO

Susan Mistler, King Philip North Middle School, Norfolk, MA

Cathy Riendeau, King Philip North Middle School, Norfolk, MA

Kent Roberts, Colville Junior High School, Colville, WA

Janet Steuart, Liberty Middle School, Tampa, FL

Jamie Wilfert, King Philip North Middle School, Norfolk, MA

We are further indebted to the following teachers for a thorough review of Chapter 10, including the activities:

William Atherton, Wellesley Middle School, Wellesley, MA
Reed Cutting, Marblehead, MA
Douglas Hardy, Robert H. Adams Middle School, Holliston, MA
Jamie Wilfert, King Philip North Middle School, Norfolk, MA

February 2005

Uri Haber-Schaim
Peter Gendel
H. Graden Kirksey
Harold A. Pratt

Contents

To The Student

In all likelihood, your experience in this course will be more satisfying than that in previous science courses.

You will be spending a considerable portion of your class time doing experiments to understand first-hand how nature behaves. To arrive at reliable experimental results requires the collection of a large amount of data. You will do this by sharing your team's data with the entire class and drawing conclusions jointly. A well-kept notebook will be of great help in organizing your work and improving your learning.

Direct experimenting will not be your only source of information. All through your life you will be learning from the experience of others transmitted through the written word. Being able to read science is a valuable skill. This course will help you to acquire it.

Finally, knowledge is truly useful when you can apply it to new situations. The many problems between sections and at the end of each chapter will help you sharpen your problem-solving skills and build a solid foundation of science content and skills for future learning.

The Authors

1 Volume and Mass

There are many ways to begin the study of physical science. We shall begin with a simple experiment that produces some surprising results. The experiment will raise some questions. At the same time, you will learn very useful laboratory skills.

E X P E R I M E N T

1.1 Heating Baking Soda

What do you think will happen if you heat some baking soda in a test tube? Will the baking soda change color? Will anything come out of the test tube? Before you read on, try to predict what will happen and be prepared to explain on what you base your prediction.

①Put some baking soda into a dry Pyrex test tube to a height of about 0.5 cm. In case a gas is produced, it will be useful to be able to collect it. ②You can do that with the apparatus shown in Figure 1.1. The bent glass tube may already have been inserted into the rubber stopper. If you have to insert the tube yourself, look closely at Figure 1.2 and its caption for useful advice on how to do it safely.

Figure 1.1

The apparatus used in heating baking soda. To be sure that no water will spill during the experiment, fill the container only up to the marker. ③Fill the bottle to the top and hold your hand over the mouth of the bottle while inverting it and placing it in the container. The rubber band helps to hold the bottle in place. Finally, insert the rubber tube all the way up to the bottom of the inverted bottle.

After your teacher has checked your setup, you may begin heating the baking soda over either a microburner or an alcohol burner. Look at Figure 1.3 to see how the flame on either burner should appear.

⚠ **CAUTION: Always wear safety glasses when you use a burner or work with gases.**

Figure 1.2
Lubricate the glass tube with glycerine or water before pushing it into the stopper. Hold the tube with a towel as close to the stopper as possible while pushing it in. This will prevent the tube from hurting you in case it breaks.

Figure 1.3
The proper size and color of the flame for a microburner (left) and for an alcohol burner.

Watch the test tube and collecting bottle as the baking soda heats up.

- What do you observe at the bottom of the test tube? Near the top?*
- Does a gas collect in the inverted bottle?

When it appears that no further changes are taking place, pull the rubber tube completely out of the water while the flame is still on. Only then turn off the flame. (Why is the sequence important?)

⚠ **CAUTION: Do not blow out the flame of a microburner; turn the valve at the gas jet.**

Even without measuring, you can see that there is more gas in the bottle than there was air in the test tube. To make sure of this, we heated an empty test tube connected to the same collecting bottle shown in Figure 1.1. All the air that was driven out of the heated test tube shows up as the bubble shown in Figure 1.4.

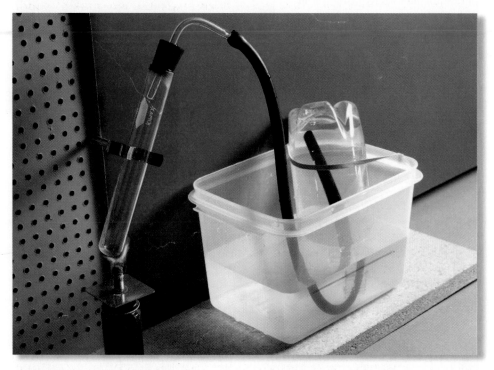

Figure 1.4

The result of heating an empty test tube for a few minutes. Clearly, the gas in your experiment was not just air from the test tube.

*Answer all bulleted questions in complete sentences. Restate enough of the information in the question so that it is clear which question is being answered.

- From where, do you think, did the gas come?
- From where did the droplets on the test tube come?

As far as you can tell by looking, the baking soda in the test tube remained unchanged. But did it really? You are going to answer this question with a simple test.

First let the test tube in which you heated the baking soda cool down. Then put about an equal amount of baking soda in a second test tube. Pour some tea into each of the two test tubes (about a quarter tube will do). Gently shake both test tubes or use a stirring rod to dissolve the powders. You have treated the content of the two test tubes equally.

- Is the color of the liquid in the two test tubes the same?
- If the color is different, can the white powder in the test tube that you heated still be baking soda? Why or why not?

Can you get the baking soda back by mixing all the substances that you have collected? Were these substances there all the time, or were they formed by heating? How can you compare the amounts of solid, liquid, and gas that you got from heating baking soda?

In order to answer these questions, you will do experiments. These experiments, in turn, will raise new questions. We shall start in the next section with the last question: How can we compare amounts of solids, liquids, and gases?

1. **Why do you think baking soda is used in baking?**

2. **List some tools that you have used**
   a. **to extend your vision to see distant objects.**
   b. **to extend your vision to see very small objects.**
   c. **to tell how hot something is.**

1.2 Volume

Suppose that you have some pennies stacked one on top of another in several piles, and that you want to know how many pennies are in each pile. The obvious thing to do is to count them. If you had to count the pennies in many piles, you could speed up the counting in the following way: Make a scale like that shown in Figure 1.5 (on the next page), marking it off in spaces equal to the thickness of one penny. You can then place this scale along-side each pile and read off the number of pennies.

If you want to measure the amount of copper in each pile of pennies, you first have to decide which unit to use to measure the amount of copper.

Figure 1.5

A scale for counting the number of pennies in a vertical pile. The distance between marks is the thickness of one penny.

If you choose as the unit the amount of copper in one penny, then the amount in the whole pile is expressed by the same number as the number of pennies.

Suppose, now, that you want to find out how much copper there is in a solid rectangular bar of copper. You might think of making a box that is the same size and shape as the copper bar and then counting the number of pennies needed to fill the box. This idea will not work, though, because when you place pennies next to one another in a rectangular box, there will always be some empty space between them.

A better way to measure the amount of copper in the bar is to choose a new unit, such as the volume of a small cube. Suppose you had a box the same size and shape as the copper bar, and you could fill it with cubes of copper of a size that would fit without air spaces between them. You could simply count the number of cubes to find the amount. Of course, you do not have to count each cube. If *a* cubes fit along the length of the box, *b* along the width, and *c* along the height, then the total number of cubes in the box (and bar) is $a \times b \times c$. (See Figure 1.6.) This is the amount of copper in the solid bar, expressed in units of cubes. As you probably know, this is also the *volume* of the bar, expressed in terms of the *volume* of the unit cube.

What we choose to be the length of each side of this unit cube is a matter of convenience. We shall choose a unit of length based on the *meter* (m), the international standard of the metric system. In this case, as in much of our work in this course, we shall use the *centimeter* (cm). A centimeter is 0.01 m. Our unit cube would then be the *cubic centimeter* (cm³), a small cube 1 cm on an edge.

To sum up, then, we can compare different amounts of the same substance by comparing their volumes—that is, the amounts of space they occupy. For a rectangular solid, we find that volume by measuring its three edges and calculating the product of these numbers. The volumes of solids of other regular shapes can also be calculated from measurements of their dimensions, but this requires additional knowledge of geometry.

The use of volume to compare amounts of substances is particularly convenient in the case of liquids, because liquids take the shape of their

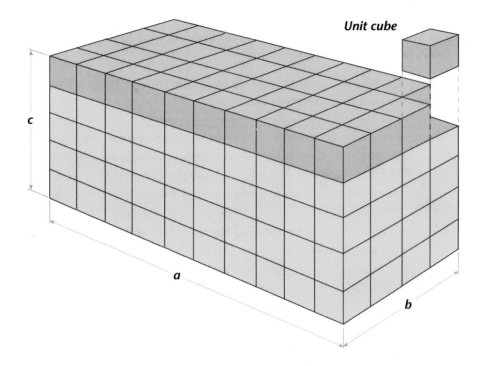

Unit cube

Figure 1.6

A bar of copper 10 cubes long, 4 cubes wide, and 5 cubes high. One layer of the bar contains 10 rows of 4 cubes each, or 10×4 cubes. There are 5 layers in the bar. Each layer contains 10×4 cubes. Therefore, the number of unit cubes in the bar is $10 \times 4 \times 5 = 200$. If the unit cube is 1 cm on an edge, the volume of the bar is 200 cm^3 (cubic centimeters). For any rectangular solid, therefore, the volume is the product of the three dimensions, $a \times b \times c$.

c

a

b

containers. Suppose you wish to compare the amounts of water in two bottles of very different shapes. You simply pour the contents of each separately into a graduated cylinder that has already been marked off with the desired units, and read the volumes (Figure 1.7). This way of measuring volume is very much like counting pennies all stacked up in a pile.

You can use the property of a liquid to take the shape of its container when you want to find the volume of a solid of irregular shape, such as a small stone. After pouring some water into a graduated cylinder and reading the volume of the water, you can submerge the stone in the water and read the combined volume of the water and the stone. The difference between the two readings is the volume of the stone.

Figure 1.7

A graduated cylinder marked off in units of volume. The cubic-centimeter marks could be made by filling the cylinder with liquid from a small cubic container, 1 cm on an edge, and making a mark at the liquid level each time a container-ful of the liquid is poured in. Many graduated cylinders are marked off in milliliters (mL). A milliliter is the same as a cubic centimeter.

3. How many cubic centimeters of water are required to fill a graduated cylinder to the 50.0 mL mark?

4. Rectangular box A has a greater volume but shorter length than rectangular box B. How is this possible?

5. A student has a large number of cubes that measure 1 cm along an edge. (If you find it helpful, use a drawing or a set of cubes to answer the following questions.)

    a. How many cubes will be needed to build a cube that measures 2 cm along an edge?

    b. How many cubes will be needed to build a cube that measures 3 cm along an edge?

    c. Express, in cubic centimeters, the volumes of the cubes built in (a) and (b).

6. One rectangular box is 30 cm long, 15 cm wide, and 10 cm deep. A second rectangular box is 25 cm long, 16 cm wide, and 15 cm deep. Which box has the larger volume?

7. Figure A shows a cone-shaped graduate used for measuring the volume of liquids. Why are the divisions not equally spaced?

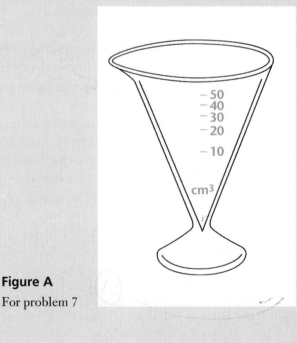

Figure A

For problem 7

1.3 Reading Scales

To measure length with a ruler, volume with a graduated cylinder, and temperature with a thermometer, you must be able to read a scale. Therefore, learning how to get all the information a scale can provide is a useful skill.

We shall begin with reading a metric ruler (Figure 1.8). The smallest divisions on such a ruler are 0.1 cm (1 mm) apart. This is a small distance indeed. Nevertheless, when the object you wish to measure has sharp edges, you can see whether the edge falls on one of the lines.

In Figure 1.9, the edge falls between two lines. It is clear that the length is between 4.8 cm and 4.9 cm. To gain more information, you can estimate the position of the edge. If you cannot tell whether the edge is closer to one line or the other, it is best to report the reading as 4.85 cm, or 48.5 mm.

If the edge is closer to the line on the left, you should report the reading as 4.82 cm or 4.83 cm. Either way, you will not be off by more than ±0.02 cm. (The symbol ± means "plus or minus.") Similarly, if you decide that the edge is closer to the line on the right, report the reading as 4.87 cm or 4.88 cm. Again, you will not be off by more than ±0.02 cm. Had you read the scale as 4.8 cm or 4.9 cm, you might have been off by as much as ±0.05 cm.

Suppose that, as far as you can tell, the edge falls on a line (as shown in Figure 1.10). Then you should report the reading as 3.20 cm. This

1 in = 2.54 cm

Figure 1.8

A metric ruler. The numbered divisions are centimeters. The small divisions are 0.1 cm, or *millimeters*.

Figure 1.9

Reading the position of the edge of an object. Here the edge falls between two of the millimeter marks.

Figure 1.10

Reading the position of the edge of an object. Here the edge falls on one of the millimeter marks.

will indicate that the reading is closer to 3.20 cm than to either 3.22 cm or 3.18 cm. Here the "0" gives us information that would have been lost had you written only "3.2 cm."

Reading the level of a liquid in a graduated cylinder poses a problem because the top of the liquid is curved. The curved surface is called a *meniscus*. Generally, we read the volume of the liquid by looking at the meniscus at eye level and reading the position of its lowest part. Measurements of volume can be reported to the nearest half of a division.

8. **The scale in Figure B is in centimeters.**

Figure B
For problem 8

a. **Estimate the positions of arrows *e* and *f* in Figure B(a) to the nearest 0.1 cm. Can you estimate their positions to 0.01 cm?**
b. **Estimate the positions of arrows *x* and *y* in Figure B(b) to the nearest 0.01 cm. Can you estimate their positions to 0.001 cm?**
c. **Why should you report the positions of the arrows in part (b) to the nearest 0.01 cm and not to the nearest 0.1 cm?**

9. **What fractions of a cubic centimeter do the smallest divisions on each of the graduated cylinders in Figure C represent? Express your answer in decimal form.**

Figure C
For problem 9

Little hashes in (a)
1 cm³

10. **What is the level of the liquid in Figure D(a) to half a division? In Figure D(b) to half a division?**

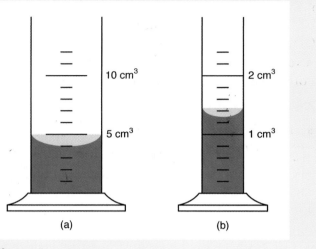

Figure D

For problem 10

11. **Three students reported the length of a pencil as 12 cm, 12.0 cm, and 12.00 cm. Do all three readings contain the same information?**

12. **What advantage is there to making graduated cylinders narrow and tall rather than short and wide?**

E X P E R I M E N T

1.4 Measuring Volume by Displacement of Water

A granular solid like sand, although it does not flow as well as a liquid, can be measured by the same method. Suppose you have some sand in a cup. To find how much space the sand takes up, you could simply pour the sand into a graduated cylinder. But does the mark the sand reaches to on the scale of the cylinder really show the volume of the sand? What about the air spaces between the loosely packed grains? The graduated cylinder really measures the combined volume of the sand plus the air spaces. However, you can do a simple experiment to find the volume of the sand alone.

Pour some sand into a dry graduated cylinder until it is about two-thirds full.

1 • What is the volume reading on the scale?

Now pour the sand into a beaker, and pour water into the graduated cylinder until it is about one-third full. Record the volume of the water, and then add the sand to the water.

2 • What is the volume of the sand plus the water?

3 • What is the volume of the sand alone?

4 • What is the volume of the air space(s) in the sand?

5 • What fraction of the dry sand is just air space? Express your answer in decimal form.

The experiment you have just done shows that we must be careful when we talk about the volume of a sample of a dry substance like sand. We must say how the volume was measured. If you have a bag of dry sand and want to know how many quart bottles it will fill, you need to know its volume dry. But if you want to know the volume of sand alone, not sand plus air space(s), then you must use a procedure like that in the experiment you have just done. You must measure the volume by liquid displacement.

Whenever we measure the volume of a solid by displacement of water, we make an assumption. We assume that the volumes of the solid alone and of the water alone add up to the volume of the solid and water together. This assumption may or may not be correct, depending on the kind of solid we have. For example, suppose you measure the volume of a few chunks of rock salt by the displacement of water. You will see that the total volume of rock salt and water becomes less as the salt dissolves. (See Figure 1.11.)

13. Adding a stone to a graduated cylinder containing 25.0 cm³ of water raises the water level in the cylinder to the 32.0 cm³ mark. What is the volume of the stone?

14. The volume of a marble is 1.0 cm³. Of the following choices, which tells how many identical marbles are needed to fill an empty graduated cylinder to the 100 cm³ mark?

   A. 100   B. More than 100   C. Less than 100

15. A volume of 50 cm³ of dry sand is added to 30 cm³ of water for a total volume of 60 cm³.

   a. What is the volume of water that does *not* go into air spaces between the sand particles?

Figure 1.11

(a) A test tube containing only water, and another test tube containing water to which two pieces of rock salt have just been added. (b) and (c) The same test tubes 15 and 30 minutes later, after the salt has begun to dissolve. Notice the decrease in the total volume of the rock salt and water, as shown by the water level in the narrow glass tube. The test tube containing the salt was shaken several times to speed up the dissolving.

   b. What is the volume of water that does fill air spaces between the sand particles?
   c. What is the volume of the air spaces between the particles in the dry sand?
   d. What is the volume of the sand particles alone?
   e. What fraction of the total volume of the dry sand is sand particles? Express your answer in decimal form.

16. How would you measure the volume of granulated sugar?

17. How would you measure the volume of a cork stopper?

20cm³

1.5 Mass: The Equal-Arm Balance

The experiment shown in Figure 1.11 strongly suggests that volume is not always a good measure of the amount of a substance. In this section, we shall discuss yet another difficulty with the use of volume to measure the amount of a substance.

If you have ever pumped up a bicycle tire with air, you know that a gas is very compressible. As you push more and more gas into the tire, its volume remains almost unchanged. Does this mean that the amount of gas in the tire remains almost unchanged, too? If you compressed the gas obtained from heating baking soda by forcing it into a container of smaller volume, would there be less of the gas?

The limitations of volume as a measure of the amount of matter must have been known to people many centuries ago. They developed a method for measuring the amounts of different substances independently of their volumes. From an Egyptian tomb several thousand years old, archaeologists have recovered a little balance arm of carved stone (Figure 1.12 (a)), with carefully made stone masses (Figure 1.12(b)). It was almost surely used, at the very dawn of history, for the careful measurement of gold dust. Goldsmiths knew even then that the balance was the best way to determine the amount of solid gold they had.

Figure 1.12(a)

This balance, the earliest one known, comes from a prehistoric grave at Naqada, Egypt, and may be 7,000 years old. It uses limestone masses and has a red limestone beam 8.5 cm long. The balance is shown at its true size. (*Courtesy of Science Museum, London*)

The balance was hung by the upper loop so that the horizontal bar was divided exactly into two arms of equal length. With no objects suspended from either arm, the balance bar would hang horizontally. An object hung from the loop on the end of one arm could be balanced by hanging some other objects from the end of the other arm.

No doubt, in using the balance, people soon learned that the bar would remain horizontal even though there were drastic changes in the shapes of the objects being balanced. Cutting up a chunk of iron into a number of pieces or filing it into a pile of small grains does not affect the

Figure 1.12(b)

Some standard masses in units of beqa (BEK-ah) found in pre-historic graves in Egypt. The letters and numbers on these four masses were placed there by archaeologists. *(Courtesy of Science Museum, London)*

balance. A balance responds to something quite independent of the form of an object. What it responds to we call *mass*.

Suppose a piece of gold balances a piece of wood, and the piece of wood balances a piece of brass. Then we say that the masses of all three are equal. If something else balances the piece of brass, it also balances the wood and the gold and therefore has the same mass. The equal-arm balance gives us a way of comparing the masses of objects of any kind, regardless of shape, of color, or of what substance they are made.

A modern equal-arm balance such as you may be using is shown in Figure 1.13. The standard unit of mass being used with this balance is the *gram* (g), a unit of mass in the metric system.

The international standard of mass in the metric system is a carefully made cylinder of platinum kept at Sèvres, France, near Paris. This cylinder has a mass of 1 *kilogram* (kg), or 1,000 g. All other kilogram masses are compared, directly or indirectly, with the standard whenever high precision is required. If you were to place an object with a mass of 1 kilogram on a supermarket scale, the scale would read 2.2 pounds.

Figure 1.13

An equal-arm laboratory balance. The object to be massed is placed on the pan at the left. The standard gram masses are placed on the pan at the right. The tip of the pointer is at the middle of the scale on the base.

18. Suppose two objects with different shapes were hung from opposite ends of an equal-arm balance. The bar remained horizontal. Which of the following statements about the properties of the objects are true?

    A. The volumes of the objects are the same.

    B. The masses of the objects are the same

    C. The objects are made up of the same substance.

    D. The colors of the objects are the same.

19. For each of the following objects, tell whether you would use a count, a volume measurement, or a mass measurement to describe the capacity of the object. Explain.

    a. Elevator

    b. Stadium

    c. Bridge

    d. Bus

    e. Water tank

    f. Freight car

    g. Theater

    h. Saucepan

20. Are items you buy at a store measured more often by volume or by mass? Give some examples.

21. What is your mass in kilograms?

1.6 Unequal-Arm Balances

An alternative to an equal-arm balance with a collection of standard masses is a balance with a pan on one side of the support and a beam with a rider on the other side (Figure 1.14). By trial, we can move the rider along the beam until we find a location near the supporting wedge where the beam is balanced, as shown in Figure 1.14. We mark this position of the rider "zero." Suppose we add a one-gram mass to the pan. We find that we have to move the rider out to a new location in order to balance the beam again. We mark this new position "one." If we add another gram mass to the pan, we must move the rider farther along the beam to balance the objects. We mark the new position as "two." We continue adding gram masses one at a time, moving the rider and marking the new location "three," "four," and so on until we reach the end of the beam. We find that all our marks are equally spaced along the beam (Figure 1.15). This procedure is called *calibrating* the balance.

Figure 1.14

An unequal-arm balance with the rider in the zero position.

Figure 1.15

The same balance as in Figure 1.14 with a 5-g standard mass on
the pan. Marks 1–5 are shown.

We can make a balance that has two beams, each with a rider of a different mass. The heavier rider lets us mass heavier objects. (We shall abbreviate "to find the mass of" to the verb "mass.") The lighter rider lets us make a more precise reading.

Figure 1.16

The top of a common balance in a physician's office. The scale is shown in both kilograms and pounds. *(Courtesy Detecto, a Division of Cardinal Scale Mfg., Co.)*

Such unequal-arm balances are very common. You probably have weighed yourself on one in your physician's office or in your school's health clinic (Figure 1.16). On such balances, the "beam" is not a single bar but instead is made of several parts. When you do experiments for this course, you may very well use an unequal-arm balance with four beams and four riders (Figure 1.17). Any manufactured unequal-arm balance has been pre-calibrated at the factory in the same way as we described above, so the calibration marks cannot be changed.

Since unequal-arm balances normally have only one pan, they are often called "single-pan balances."

Figure 1.17

A single-pan balance with four beams and four riders.

22. What is the advantage of using an unequal-arm balance rather than an equal-arm balance when massing a person?

1.7 Electronic Balances

An electronic balance (Figure 1.18) does not look at all like a balance. A balance compares the mass of the object on the pan with standard masses. The standard masses are placed either on a second pan or as riders on beams. An electronic balance has neither a second pan nor beams carrying riders.

If you press down gently on the pan of an electronic balance, you will notice that the pan moves very slightly. The change in the position of the pan depends on the mass that is placed on it. This change in position is translated by the electronic circuit into a number shown on the digital display. We must first calibrate an electronic balance with a known mass before we can use it to measure unknown masses.

Electronic balances, or top loaders, as they are often called, have two advantages. First, it takes only seconds to mass an object. Thus, many teams in the laboratory can share one balance. Second, in many experiments you will need to find the mass of a liquid or powder in a container. A top loader can subtract the mass of the container and give you the mass of its contents directly. To use this feature, you press the *tare* button with the empty container on the pan. Then you mass the filled container.

Top loaders are delicate instruments and must be handled with care. In particular, use them only in the range for which they were designed. Your balance should probably not be loaded with more than 100 g.

Figure 1.18

An electronic balance with the 100-g calibration mass on the pan.

EXPERIMENT

1.8 The Sensitivity of a Balance

If you mass the same object several times, will you find the same mass each time? And a related question: Will you detect the addition of small known masses on the balance, no matter how small they are? The purpose of this experiment is to find out how much you can trust your balance in answering such questions.

How you get the balance ready for the experiment will depend on the kind of balance available in your classroom. If you are working with an equal-arm balance, skip the next two paragraphs. If you are working with a single-pan balance, read the next paragraph but skip the following one. If you have a top loader, skip only the next paragraph.

A single-pan balance, like the one pictured in Figure 1.17, must be "zeroed" before each use. To zero a balance means to adjust it to balance correctly under a single condition. In that condition, nothing is on its pan and all riders are moved to the extreme left of their beams so they are at zero. The knob used to make this adjustment is shown in Figure 1.19 at the upper left of the balance. Be sure to zero your balance while it is standing on a steady, level surface.

An electronic top-loading balance, like the one in Figure 1.18, should be placed on a steady, level surface and "zeroed" before it is used. To zero a balance means to adjust it to display "zero" when there

Figure 1.19

A close-up of a single-pan balance.
The zero-adjustment knob is at the
left end.

is zero mass on its pan. The procedure for doing this is easily accomplished for top-loading balances, but differs from model to model. Your teacher will tell you how to zero the top-loading balance that you will be using.

Let us return to the first question: If you mass the same object several times, will you find the same mass each time? Mass two objects, such as a penny and a rubber stopper, alternately several times. To avoid being influenced by your previous results, have your lab partner read and record the results. Using two objects will make it necessary for you to change the settings. If you work with either an equal-arm balance or a single-pan balance, try to read the rider position as accurately as possible. Change roles with your lab partner, and then compare your results.

- Does your balance give reproducible results to the nearest 0.01 g? the nearest 0.001 g, or something in between?

Now for the second question: How much must the masses of two objects differ before your balance is able to distinguish between them? To obtain small, known masses, you will cut a group of smaller squares from a large square of graph paper that you have massed. Begin by neatly cutting a square of graph paper 20 squares along an edge. This large square is made up of 400 small squares.

Estimate the mass of the large square to the nearest 0.1 g. You can write your estimate on the square and compare the result with your classmates'. Now mass the large square.

- What is the mass of your large square of graph paper?

Calculate the mass of a single small square. For the purpose of this experiment, it will be convenient to have groups of squares with a mass between 0.003 and 0.007 g.

- How many of your small squares are in a group that has a mass between 0.003 and 0.007 g?
- What is the mass of such a group of small squares?

Now cut ten of these groups of small squares. With a penny or rubber stopper already balanced, add the groups of small squares one by one and observe the effect on the balance.

- How many groups of small squares did you have to add before the balance gave you a reliable response?

★ The smallest change in mass that a balance can detect in a reproducible way is called the *sensitivity* of the balance.

- What is the sensitivity of your balance?

23. A rectangle made from two squares of graph paper has a mass of 0.0045 g. The results of adding 10 such rectangles one at a time to an electronic balance are given below along with the mass readings on the scale. (N = no change in reading; Y = change in reading).

Initial mass on the scale = 2.64 g	
1. N	6. N
2. N	7. N
3. Y 2.65 g	8. Y 2.67 g
4. N	9. N
5. Y 2.66 g	10. Y 2.68 g

Based on these results, what should you report for the sensitivity of the balance?

24. Karen massed an object three times, using the same equal-arm balance and gram masses. Her results were: 18.324 g, 18.308 g, and 18.342 g. How could she best report the mass of the object?

25. Five students in turn used the same balance to measure the mass of a small dish. None knew what results the others obtained. The masses they found are given in the table below.

Student	Mass (g)
1	3.752
2	3.755
3	3.752
4	3.756
5	3.760

a. Can you tell whether any student made an incorrect measurement?
b. Do you think there is anything wrong with the balance?
c. What do you think is the best way to report the mass of the dish?

26. Susan massed an object three times, using the same single-pan balance. Her results were: 21.420 g, 21.425 g, and 21.410 g. How could she best report the mass of the object?

27. Five students in turn used the same single-pan balance to measure the mass of a small dish. None knew what results the others obtained. The masses they found are given in the table below.

Student	Mass (g)
1	4.360
2	4.370
3	4.365
4	4.360
5	4.355

a. Can you tell whether any student made an incorrect measurement?
b. Do you think there is anything wrong with the balance?
c. What do you think is the best way to report the mass of the dish?

28. Five students in turn used the same electronic balance to measure the mass of a small dish. None knew the results of the others. The masses are given in the table below.

Student	Mass (g)
1	4.36
2	4.37
3	4.36
4	4.37
5	4.36

a. Can you tell whether any student made an incorrect measurement?
b. Do you think there is anything wrong with the balance?
c. What do you think is the best way to report the mass of the dish?

29. Suppose the volume of a piece of glass is measured by displacement of water and by displacement of burner fuel. How would the two measurements compare?

30. In determining the volume of a rectangular box, five cubes were found to fit exactly along one edge, and four cubes to fit exactly along another edge. However, after six horizontal layers had been stacked in the box, a space at the top was left unfilled.

    a. If the height of the space was half the length of an edge of a unit cube, what was the volume of the box?
    b. If the height of the space was 0.23 of the length of an edge of a unit cube, what was the volume of the box?

31. What is the total number of cubes that will fit in the space enclosed by the dashed lines in Figure E? Is there more than one way to find an answer?

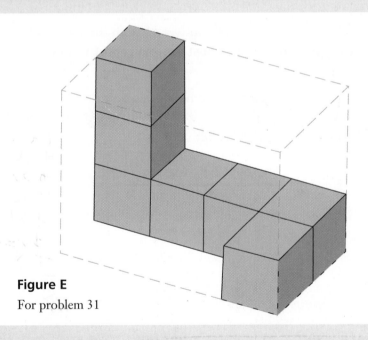

Figure E
For problem 31

32. In an experiment in which the volume of dry sand is measured by the displacement of water, the sand was slightly wet to begin with. What effect would this have on the volume of air space that was calculated? On the percentage of the volume that was air space?

33. a. How would you measure the volume of a sponge?

    b. What have you actually measured by your method?

    c. Does this differ from your measurement of the volume of sand?

34. Fuel oil usually is sold by the gallon, gas for cooking by the cubic foot, and coal by the ton. What are the advantages of selling the first two by volume and the last by mass?

35. In the following list of ingredients for a recipe, which are measured by volume, which by mass, and which by other means?

1½ pounds ground chuck	pinch of pepper
1 medium-size onion	3 drops steak sauce
½ cup chopped green pepper	oregano to taste
4 slices day-old bread	3 tablespoons oil
1 teaspoon salt	1 1-pound can tomato sauce

36. a. What is the volume of an aluminum cube with edges that are 10 cm long?

    b. What is the mass of the aluminum cube? (One cubic centimeter of aluminum has a mass of 2.7 g.)

37. One cubic centimeter of gold has a mass of 19 g.

    a. What is the mass of a gold bar 1.0 cm × 2.0 cm × 25 cm?

    b. How many of these bars could you carry?

38. Suppose that you took home an equal-arm balance. When you were ready to use it, you found that you had forgotten a set of gram masses.

    a. How could you make a set of uniform masses from materials likely to be found in your home?

    b. How could you relate your unit of mass to a gram?

39. Suppose you balance a piece of modeling clay on the balance. Then you reshape it. Will it still balance? If you shape it into a hollow sphere, will it still balance?

40. Estimate in grams the mass of a watch. Now find the mass of a nickel (5¢) on your balance. Estimate the mass of the watch again. Did you change your estimate? Does knowing the mass of a nickel help you to better estimate your own mass? Why?

41. How could a person easily tell which letters had four and which five pages without opening the envelopes? What assumption did you make in arriving at your answer?

Themes for Short Essays

1. Suppose you are employed as a technical writer by a company that manufactures graduated cylinders. Printed instructions are to be included in packages sent out by the company. Write instructions telling customers how to use the cylinders correctly to measure the volumes of liquids.

2. A friend wants to use your balance during the summer. Write a complete set of instructions for her so that she will be able to do so successfully on her own without anybody being present to help her.

Mass Changes in Closed Systems

EXPERIMENT *physical*

2.1 The Mass of Dissolved Salt

In Section 1.4, you learned that as salt dissolves in water, the combined volume of salt plus water decreases. This leads us to ask whether the mass also decreases when salt is dissolved in water.

Pour about 2 g of salt into the cap of a small plastic bottle, and carefully put it aside. Pour water into the plastic bottle until it is about two-thirds full. Find the total mass of the bottle, water, cap, and salt when all are on the balance together but the salt and water are not mixed.

Carefully pour the salt into the bottle, and put on the cap. Shake the bottle occasionally to speed up the dissolving of the salt. After the salt has dissolved, mass the capped bottle.

- Taking into consideration the sensitivity of the balance, what do you conclude about the mass of salt and water as the salt dissolves?

Answering this question calls for a comparison between two mass measurements, before and after dissolving. A good way to do that is to subtract the earlier value from the later value. This difference is called the *change* in mass. Suppose that the earlier mass was 28.36 g and the later mass was 28.37 g. Then the change is

$$28.37 \text{ g} - 28.36 \text{ g} = 0.01 \text{ g}.$$

In this example, the later mass was greater than the earlier one. Suppose the earlier mass were 26.12 g and the later mass were 26.10 g. The change would still be calculated by subtracting the earlier value from the later value:

$$26.10 \text{ g} - 26.12 \text{ g} = -0.02 \text{ g}.$$

Thus, change is expressed by a signed number; it can be positive, zero, or negative.

Your measurements sum up the result of a single experiment. To have more confidence in your conclusion, you would have to repeat the experiment several times to be sure that you have not spilled any salt or made an error in reading a scale. Many repetitions would use up much time and would be boring. So, instead of asking you to repeat this experiment, we shall bring together the results of all the experiments done by the whole class. We shall follow the same procedure with other experiments.

The first step is to display the data from all stations on the chalkboard. For future reference, copy that table in your notebook.

- Considering the sensitivity of the balance, and the results of the entire class, what does your class conclude about the mass of salt and water as the salt dissolves?

• Can you suggest any reasons why all the members of the class do not find the same change in mass?

1. Here are the results of several mass measurements. In which is the change stated correctly?

	Before	After	Change
A.	42.67 g	42.65 g	+0.02 g
B.	69.05 g	65.05 g	0
C.	43.12 g	43.22 g	+0.10 g
D.	43.10 g	42.95 g	−1.15 g
E.	25.64 g	25.61 g	−0.03 g

2. Do you need to know the individual masses of the samples of water and salt in order to measure the change in mass when the two samples are mixed?

3. In Experiment 2.1, The Mass of Dissolved Salt, how could you recover the dissolved salt? How do you think its mass would compare with the mass of dry salt you started with?

4. If the change in mass in Experiment 2.1, The Mass of Dissolved Salt, were −0.0001 g, would you have observed this change using your balance?

5. a. In daily language we express the sign (plus or minus) of a change by using different words. For example, Elizabeth gained 1 kg, Tom lost 2 kg. Express these statements in terms of change in mass.

    b. In the morning the temperature rose from 10°C to 14°C. In the afternoon the temperature fell from 16°C to 11°C. What were the changes in temperature in the morning and in the afternoon?

2.2 Histograms

You probably have heard the proverb "a picture is worth a thousand words." Replace "words" by "numbers" and you have a statement that is just as valid. To see for yourself, consider the data in Table 2.1 on the next page. They were taken by a large class.

Table 2.1 Class Data from Experiment 2.1, The Mass of Dissolved Salt

Team number	Mass before (g)	Mass after (g)	Change in mass (g)	Team number	Mass before (g)	Mass after (g)	Change in mass (g)
1	32.17	32.24	+ 0.07	11	31.31	31.26	– 0.05
2	29.57	29.36	– 0.21	12	32.55	32.38	– 0.17
3	28.67	28.67	0	13	32.26	32.21	– 0.05
4	38.02	38.02	0	14	34.29	34.27	– 0.02
5	27.67	27.64	– 0.03	15	31.43	31.39	– 0.04
6	31.55	31.55	0	16	31.86	31.86	0
7	31.45	31.43	– 0.02	17	30.86	30.87	+ 0.01
8	35.12	35.12	0	18	30.29	30.29	0
9	31.45	31.45	0	19	29.14	29.15	+ 0.01
10	28.67	28.65	– 0.02	20	30.86	30.64	– 0.22

All the data are in the table, but it is hard to grasp the content of the table all at once. Are the results of teams 1 and 2 typical of the entire class? Are the results of other teams close to those of either of them? Are the results of other teams somewhere in between the results of teams 1 and 2?

A glance at the "Change in mass" columns will show that the value of the change in mass that occurs most often is zero. There are also a few entries of +0.01 g and –0.02 g. Are they significantly different from zero? The change in mass was calculated by subtracting the mass before dissolving from the mass after dissolving. Each of these measurements has an uncertainty of ± 0.01 g. For example, the results of team 3 could have been 28.67 g before and 28.66 g after, yielding a change of –0.01 g. To be able to draw conclusions from the data, we need to present them in a way that will emphasize an overall trend, with less detail.

Here is a simple way of doing just that. Imagine we arrange a number of bins or boxes marked "–0.03 to –0.01," "–0.01 to +0.01," and so on. Each team in the class writes its result for the change in mass on a card and deposits the card in the bin labeled with the appropriate interval (Figure 2.1). What should be done with values that are on the boundary between two bins? The simplest solution is to put them always in the bin to the right, as was done in Figure 2.1.

Once all the cards have been placed in the bins, we count the cards in each bin and plot a bar graph of the results. Of course, we do not need real bins. We can use squares on graph paper instead. As with all graphs, it is a good idea to find the largest and smallest values first in order to know how to mark the scale on the horizontal axis (Figure 2.2).

Figure 2.1

"Bins" for depositing data. The numbers in the upper row show the centers of the intervals represented by the bins. The ones in the lower row show the boundaries.

Now we can go through Table 2.1 and mark a square for each value in the table. If a value has already appeared, we draw its square on top of the one below it. The final result is shown in Figure 2.3 (on the next page). The height of each column tell us the number of measurements that belong in each bin. A plot like Figure 2.3 that presents data by the number of times a value appears in an interval is called a *histogram*.

A histogram enables us to make several immediate observations. Most of the data are bunched around zero, with zero being the most frequent result. Some regions on both sides of zero have no data at all. But of the few readings far from zero, there are more on the left, indicating a loss, than on the right, indicating a gain.

Figure 2.2

The starting points of a histogram: fitting the data on both ends of the horizontal axis.

Figure 2.3

A histogram of the data in Table 2.1, with an interval width of 0.02 g and with zero at the center of an interval.

How would the data of Table 2.1 appear had we placed the zero point at the border between two intervals (Figure 2.4)? Following the convention that a border-value is placed in the interval to the right, the resulting histogram is shown in Figure 2.5. The histograms in Figures 2.3 and 2.5 have the same general appearance. However, the histogram shown in Figure 2.5 seems to suggest that the most frequent result is a small gain in mass. This apparent conclusion is the result of having chosen the zero point at the border between intervals, thereby shifting many values to the right. Thus, to avoid drawing erroneous conclusions from histograms, try to set the borders between intervals so that frequent values fit into intervals rather than on their borders.

Figure 2.4

The arrangement of bins with the zero point at a boundary.

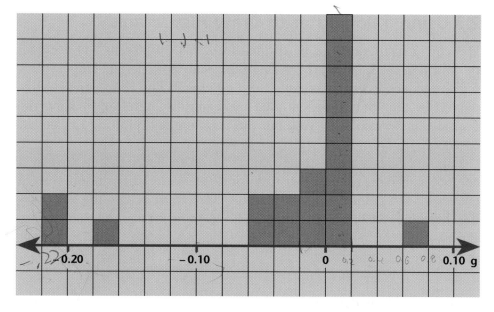

Figure 2.5
A complete histogram of the data in Table 2.1, with an interval width of 0.02 g and with zero at a boundary.

6. Consider a histogram that has an interval whose boundaries are −0.01 g and +0.01 g. Which of the values (in grams) given below should be counted in this interval?
   A. -0.002
   B. -0.001
   C. 0
   D. +0.006
   E. +0.01
   F. +0.02

7. a. What is the interval immediately to the left of the interval containing zero in Figure 2.1?
   b. Identify the teams whose data appear in this column.

8. a. What interval is immediately to the right of zero in Figure 2.5?
   b. Identify the teams whose data appear in this column.
   c. Identify the teams whose data are in the last column on the left in Figure 2.5.

9. a. Draw a histogram of the data in Table 2.1. Use intervals with a width of 0.01 g and place zero at the center of an interval.
   b. If you drew the histogram correctly, the interval immediately to the left of zero should be empty. Why?
   c. This observation is lost in Figure 2.3. Therefore, is the new histogram better than the one shown in Figure 2.3? Explain your answer.

2.3 Using a Computer to Draw Histograms

Drawing a histogram can be divided into two main steps: (1) deciding the width of the bins and the value of the center of one bin, and (2) placing the values in the bins and counting them. The first step requires judgment, the second step is quite mechanical. Therefore, making the decisions is best done by you, but the counting and plotting can be left to a computer.

Figure 2.6 shows a histogram of the data in Table 2.1 created by a computer using a program written for *IPS*. Notice that the number of entries in each column must be read on the vertical axis on the left. Having the computer do the counting and drawing is to your advantage. You can try different histograms in a short time and find the one that in your opinion best summarizes the data.

Figure 2.6

A computer-generated histogram of the data in Table 2.1.

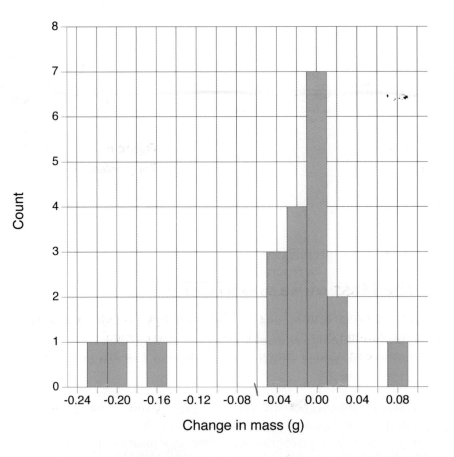

10. a. **What is the width of an interval in the histogram shown in Figure 2.6?**
    b. **Is zero at the center or at the border of the interval?**

11. **Figures A and B also show histograms made from the data in Table 2.1. In each of these histograms,**
    a. **what is the width of the intervals?**
    b. **is zero at the center of an interval or at a border?**

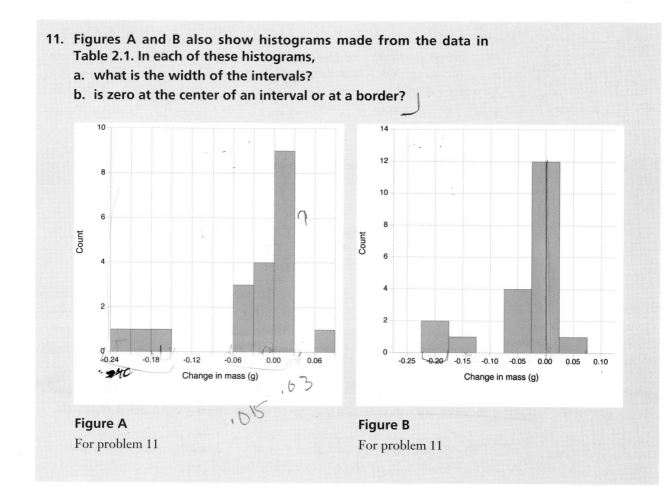

Figure A
For problem 11

Figure B
For problem 11

EXPERIMENT

2.4 The Mass of Ice and Water

Here is another process involving a volume change. When ice melts, it contracts—its volume decreases. Does its mass also change?

Put an ice cube in a small container and put the lid on the container.

• What is the total mass of the ice and the container?

After all the ice has melted (if the container is not transparent, you can tell by shaking it), mass again.

• Do you notice any condensation of water on the outside of the container?

• If so, what should you do about it?

• From a histogram of class data, what do you conclude about change in mass when ice melts?

12. Between the time that a lab group measured the mass of the ice before melting and the mass of the ice after melting, a second lab group spilled a few drops of water on the balance. Which of the following statements describes the effect of this spill on the calculated change in mass?

A. The calculated change in mass would be greater.

B. The calculated change in mass would be smaller.

C. The calculated change in mass would not be affected.

EXPERIMENT *chemical*
2.5 The Mass of Copper and Sulfur

The changes you have examined so far were quite mild. A more dramatic change in matter takes place when sulfur and copper are heated together. Does the total mass change when these substances are heated together?

Put about 2 g of granular copper and about 1 g of sulfur in a test tube.

⚠ CAUTION: Do *not* use copper powder or copper dust. Always wear safety glasses when you use a burner.

Mix with a glass rod or shake gently. Close the end with a piece of rubber sheet held in place by a rubber band. Record the total mass of the closed tube. Heat the mixture gently until it begins to glow; then remove the flame immediately.

⚠ CAUTION: Do *not* touch the test tube until it has cooled.

- Has the total mass of copper and sulfur changed?

   Describe the appearance of the material in the test tube.

- Do you think the substance in the bottom is sulfur, copper, or a new substance?

13. The following data were recorded in an experiment in which copper and sulfur were made to react.

	Mass (g)
Tube and cover	20.484
Tube, cover, copper, and sulfur before reaction	23.440
Tube, cover, and products after reaction	23.386

a. What is the mass of the substances before the reaction?

b. What is the apparent change in mass of the reacting substances?

c. What is the apparent percentage change in mass of the reacting substances?

14. A test tube containing 4.00 g of iron and 2.40 g of sulfur was heated in a manner similar to that of the copper-and-sulfur experiment. Before heating, the total mass of the tube and contents measured on the balance was 36.50 g. After heating, the mass was measured again. The mass of the tube and contents was 36.48 g.

a. Do you think it reasonable that mass remained the same—was conserved—during this experiment?

b. What additional steps would you take to increase your confidence in your answer to part (a)?

EXPERIMENT

2.6 The Mass of a Gas

In this experiment, a solid and a liquid produce a gas. Is there a change in mass?

⚠ CAUTION: Be sure to use only the small *thick-walled* bottle wrapped with tape that your teacher has provided. Always wear safety glasses when you work with gases.

Fill the bottle one-third full of water, then mass the bottle, its cap, and *one-eighth* of an Alka-Seltzer tablet. Place the piece of tablet in the bottle. Immediately screw the cap on very tightly and put it back on the balance.

• Does what happens inside the bottle affect the mass of the bottle and its contents?

Slowly loosen the cap.

• Do you hear gas escaping?

Again mass the cap, the bottle, and its contents.

• What do you conclude?

2.7 The Conservation of Mass

What have the last four experiments shown? If you have worked carefully, you have found that all the changes in mass that you observed were within the experimental uncertainty of your equipment. Therefore, your results agree with the conclusion that there was no change in mass that you could measure. From these experiments alone, you cannot predict with confidence that there will be no change in mass under other circumstances. For example, if you use larger amounts of matter in the experiments and use a balance of higher sensitivity, you might measure a change greater than the range of experimental uncertainty. Then you would conclude that mass really does not remain the same. Furthermore, although you checked four rather different kinds of change, there is an endless variety of other reactions you could have tried, some even more violent than the reaction of copper and sulfur.

What would happen, for example, if you set off a small explosion inside a heavy steel case, making sure nothing escaped? The experiments you have done give no direct answer to this question. But we can make the guess that the results of these four experiments can be generalized in the following way: In all changes, mass is exactly conserved, provided nothing is added (like the water that condensed on the outside of the closed container in the experiment with ice and water) and nothing escapes (like the gas in the last experiment). An experimental setup in which these conditions are satisfied is called a *closed system*. The generalization we have just stated is known as *the law of conservation of mass*. It holds for closed systems. It has been checked to one part in a billion* for a large variety of changes. That is, experiments have been done in which a change in mass of one billionth of the total mass would have been observed if it had occurred.

Still, all this vast amount of evidence in favor of the law of conservation of mass does not prove that it will hold forever under all conditions. Surely, if someone claimed that he or she had done an experiment in which as much as one millionth of the mass disappeared or was created, we should treat the results with great suspicion. First of all, we should make many checks to determine whether there had been a leak of some sort in the apparatus from which, say, gas could escape. The chances are

---

*A billion is 1,000,000,000. Such a number is clumsy to write. Most of the zeros can be dispensed with by writing the number as 10^9 and reading it "ten to the ninth." The 9 is called an *exponent* and tells how many times we multiply 1 by 10 to get the number. For example, $1 \times 10 \times 10 = 10^2$, $1 \times 10 \times 10 \times 10 = 10^3$, and so on. We shall use this way of expressing numbers, called *powers-of-10 notation*, whenever it is convenient.

margin of error

(closed system) mass cannot be created or destroyed

lots of evidence over time = law but does not prove it will hold for all conditions that we would find such a leak. On the other hand, suppose an experiment were done in which a change in mass of one part in 100 billion was reported. We might have to conclude, after a thorough examination of the experiment, that the law of conservation of mass has its limitations, that it holds to one part in a billion but not to one part in 100 billion (10^{11}). To date, no exceptions to the law of conservation of mass have been observed.

We have seen in this chapter that volume is very often a convenient way of measuring the quantity of matter. But we have also found out that, when matter changes form (when ice melts, salt dissolves, and so on), there is often an easily measurable change in volume but no observable change in mass: mass is conserved. It is the <u>conservation of mass</u> <u>that makes</u> mass such a <u>useful measure</u> of matter.

---

15. **A student wished to add a new experiment to Chapter 2 by examining the change in mass of heated water. The mass of a beaker containing a sample of water at 20°C was found to be 109.44 g. After heating the sample to 60°C, the combined mass of the beaker and water was found to be 109.08 g. Do these results contradict the law of conservation of mass? Explain your reasoning.**

NO. DIC beaker is not a closed system

2.8 Laws of Nature

The law of conservation of mass is the first of several laws of nature that we shall study in this course. It is worthwhile to pause at this point and compare the laws of nature with the laws of society. Laws of society are legislated; that is, they are agreed upon and then enforced. If evidence is presented that you have broken such a law, you are punished. The laws of society can also be changed or repealed.

Laws of nature are different. Some laws began as lucky guesses based on a few crude experiments. Others were generalizations based on the analysis of many sophisticated experiments. Regardless of how it comes about, a person takes a risk in announcing what he or she believes to be a law of nature. Such a statement must stand the criticism and evaluation of many people doing additional experiments before it is recognized as a law of nature.

If you do an experiment that appears to violate a law of nature, you are not punished. On the contrary, if you present convincing evidence that the law is not quite true, the law is changed. Only rarely does this lead to a complete repeal of the law. In most cases, the change is a recognition of the limitation of the law.

16. There is an old saying: "What goes up, must come down." Does this express a law of nature? Why, or why not?

17. On a sunny day the sky is blue. Is this a law of nature? Why or why not?

▶ For Review, Applications, and Extensions

18. Suggest a reason for putting the lid on the small container that you used in studying the mass of ice and water.

19. In Experiment 2.4, The Mass of Ice and Water, would the mass of the container and its contents stay the same if you started with water and froze it? Try it.

20. Suppose you placed the entire setup used in Experiment 1.1, Heating Baking Soda (see Figure 1.1) on a balance and recorded the mass before and after heating. What would you expect to find?

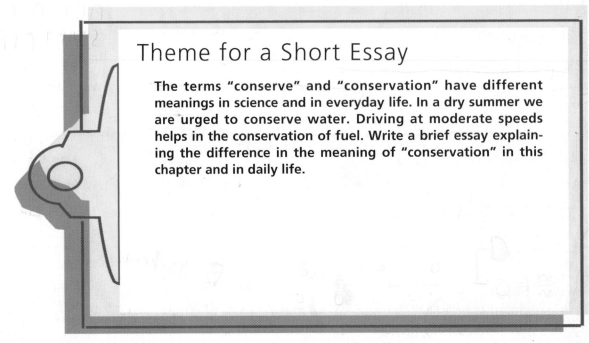

Theme for a Short Essay

The terms "conserve" and "conservation" have different meanings in science and in everyday life. In a dry summer we are urged to conserve water. Driving at moderate speeds helps in the conservation of fuel. Write a brief essay explaining the difference in the meaning of "conservation" in this chapter and in daily life.

3 Characteristic Properties

3.1 Properties of Substances and Properties of Objects

How do you know when two substances are different? It is easy enough to distinguish between wood, iron, and rock, or between water and milk; but there are other cases in which it is not so easy. Suppose that you are given two pieces of metal. Both look equally shiny and feel equally hard. Are they the same metal? Or think of samples of two liquids. Both liquids are transparent and have no smell. Are they the same or different?

To answer such questions, we shall have to do things to substances in order to reveal differences that are not directly apparent. Merely massing the two pieces of metal will not do. Two objects can be made of different materials and yet have the same mass. Think of a 100-g steel cylinder and a 100-g brass cylinder of the kind used as masses on a balance. On the other hand, two objects can have different masses and be made of the same material. For example, consider two hammers, both made of steel but one much larger and with a greater mass than the other. Mass is a property of an object. It is not a property of the substance of which the object is made.

To find out if two pieces of metal that look alike are made of the same substance, you may try to bend them. Again, one may be thick and hard to bend, and the other may be thin and easy to bend; yet they both may be made of the same substance. On the other hand, you may find that two pieces of metal of different thicknesses but made of different substances bend with equal ease. Thus, ease of bending is also a property of the object and not of the substance.

Suppose we want to find out whether two objects are made of the same substance or of different ones. We have to look for properties that are characteristic of substances and not properties of objects. In this chapter we shall concentrate on properties that show differences between substances. These we call *characteristic properties*.

1. State which words in the following descriptions refer to the substances and which refer to the objects.

   a. A sharp, heavy, shiny, stainless-steel knife

   b. A small chunk of black tar

   c. A beautifully carved wooden chair

EXPERIMENT
3.2 Mass and Volume

By now you have measured the mass and volume of different objects. Will the mass of one cubic centimeter of an object depend on its shape? Will the mass of one cubic centimeter of an object depend on the substance of which it is made?

The three long, thin cylinders shown in Figure 3.1 were cut from a uniform rod of aluminum. Using a 10-mL graduated cylinder, you can verify that each of them has a volume of 1.0 cm³.

• Do you expect the mass of these three cylinders to be the same? Why or why not? Mass the three cylinders to check your expectation.

Suppose that the aluminum rod from which the three cylinders were made was cut into cylinders twice as long.

• What would be the mass of each cylinder?
• What would be its volume?
• How can you find the mass of one cubic centimeter of such a cylinder without cutting it in half?

The three cylinders with which you have been working have the same shape. Does the mass of a piece of aluminum depend on shape or only on volume? To answer this question, you will use another aluminum cylinder. Its volume is also 1.0 cm³ and it fits into the 10-mL graduated cylinder.

Figure 3.1
Five cylinders. Each has a volume of 1.0 cm³.

- What is the mass of the short aluminum cylinder?

A piece of aluminum and a piece of brass can be cut so they have the same mass or the same volume. Can you make a piece of brass that will have both the same mass and the same volume as a piece of aluminum? To help answer this question, you can use a 1.0-cm³ brass cylinder.

- What do you find?

2. If the mass of your long aluminum rod is 2.7 g, which of the following is the mass of an aluminum rod with a volume of 3.0 cm³?
   A. 0.9 g
   B. 2.7 g
   C. 8.1 g

3. If the mass of your brass cylinder is 8.5 g, which of the following is the mass of a brass cylinder with a volume of 0.6 cm³?
   A. 5.1 g
   B. 8.5 g
   C. 14.2 g

3.3 Density

Rarely do we encounter samples of matter having exactly one unit volume (1 cm³), as you did in Experiment 3.2, Mass and Volume. In the laboratory, we usually work with samples that have a volume either larger or smaller than one unit volume. Nevertheless, we can still find the mass of a unit volume of a substance. We begin by measuring the mass and volume of any size sample of a substance. The mass of one unit volume can then be calculated from these measurements by dividing the mass of the sample by its volume.

Suppose a sample of aluminum was measured and found to have a volume of 4.8 cm³ and a mass of 13 g. We calculate the mass of a unit volume of aluminum in the following way:

$$\frac{13 \text{ g}}{4.8 \text{ cm}^3} = 2.7 \text{ g/cm}^3.$$

We calculated the mass of a unit volume by dividing mass by volume. Therefore we refer to the mass of a unit volume as "mass per unit volume." The word "per" means a division by the quantity that follows it. For example, the speed of a car is stated in miles per hour—that is, a distance measurement divided by a time measurement. The mass per unit volume of a substance is called the *density* of that substance. Density is a characteristic property. Its units are g/cm³ (grams per cubic centimeter). In the example shown above, the density of the aluminum is 2.7 g/cm³. The two statements, "The mass of 1 cm³ of aluminum is 2.7 g," and "The density of aluminum is 2.7 g/cm³" contain the same information. The second statement is shorter and is used more often.

4. A parking lot is filled with automobiles.
   a. Does the number of wheels in the lot depend upon the number of automobiles?
   b. Does the number of wheels per automobile depend upon the number of automobiles?
   c. Is the number of wheels per automobile a characteristic property of automobiles that distinguishes them from other vehicles?

5. a. Draw a graph of the number of wheels in a parking lot as a function of the number of cars.
   b. Draw a graph of the number of wheels per car as a function of the number of cars in the lot.

6. Suppose you were to plot the density of aluminum as a function of the mass of several samples of aluminum. Describe the appearance of the resulting graph.

3.4 Dividing and Multiplying Measured Numbers

When you find the density of a substance from the measured mass and volume of a sample, your calculation uses numbers of limited accuracy. For example, consider a pebble that has a mass of 12.36 g and a volume of 4.7 cm³. Here the mass is given to four digits and the volume to two. If you calculate the quotient 12.36 g/4.7 cm³ on a calculator, you get the number 2.62978723. However, not even a calculator can produce numbers that are more accurate than the data used in the calculations.

For division and multiplication, it is good to remember a simple rule of thumb: The result should have as many digits as the measured number with the fewest digits. It is always advisable to calculate one additional digit, and then round off. In the example we just saw, the density is

$$\frac{12.36 \text{ g}}{4.7 \text{ cm}^3} = 2.6 \text{ g/cm}^3.$$

The "2" and the "6" are called *significant digits*. The remaining digits in the display of the calculator are not significant and should be dropped.

If we calculate the volume of an object from its dimensions, the same rule applies. Suppose the measured dimensions of a rectangular solid are 4.82 cm, 11.05 cm, and 1.28 cm. Then the volume of the solid is correctly reported as

$$4.82 \text{ cm} \times 11.05 \text{ cm} \times 1.28 \text{ cm} = 68.2 \text{ cm}^3.$$

The volume should *not* be reported as 68.174080 cm^3.

How do we count the digits in a decimal measurement whose last digit is a zero, as in the measurement 4.20 cm? (Section 1.3 contains an explanation of why the zero is written.) In these cases, the zero is counted as a significant digit. However, in such measured numbers as 0.86 cm and 0.045 g, the zeros are not counted. Their only purpose is to locate the decimal point. Both these numbers are given to two significant digits.

7. **How many significant digits are in each of the following measurements?**

a. 4.0 cm^3	b. 78.21 g
c. 7.05 cm	d. 5.40 g
e. 0.033 m	f. 225 cm
g. 0.01 g	h. 0.930 m

8. **Do the following calculations to the proper number of digits.**

a. $\dfrac{125}{23.7}$ b. $\dfrac{20.5}{51.0}$ c. $\dfrac{0.065}{32.5}$ d. $\dfrac{1.23}{0.72}$

e. 4.72×0.52 f. 6.3×10.08

g. $1.55 \times 2.61 \times 5.3$ h. $3.01 \times 5.00 \times 25.62$

9. **Suppose the measured dimensions of a rectangle are 3.62 cm and 12.06 cm.**

a. **With a calculator, determine the area of the rectangle and report all the digits on the display.**

b. **Suppose each measurement could be off by ± 0.02 cm. Report the least and greatest possible values for the area of the rectangle. Use a calculator and report all the digits.**

c. **Which of the digits calculated in part (a) are the same as those calculated in part (b)?**

d. **Why should you report your answer to part (a) using only three digits, as suggested by the rule of thumb on page 45?**

10. Suppose that a pebble has a mass of 12.36 g and a volume of 4.7 cm³.

   a. With a calculator, determine the density of the pebble and report all the digits on the display. *2.6*

   b. Suppose the measurements could be off by ±0.01 g and ±0.01 cm³. Report the least and greatest possible values for the density of the pebble. Use a calculator and report all the digits. *2.55   2.64*

   c. Which of the digits calculated in part (b) are the same as those calculated in part (a)?

   d. Why should you report your answer to part (a) using only two digits, as suggested by the rule of thumb on page 45?

12.35
4.69

12.37
4.71

EXPERIMENT

3.5 The Density of Solids

Pick up two cubes that look alike and that have the same volume. Can you decide simply by handling them whether they have the same or different masses?

Mass the cubes on your balance.

- Which of the cubes has the greater density?

Now, just by handling them, compare the mass of each of the cubes with the mass of the slab, which has a different volume.

- Can you decide in this way if the slab is made of a different substance?

Measure the dimensions of each of the three objects as accurately as you can. Calculate the volume and then the density of each.

- Are you now able to decide whether or not the slab is made of the same substance as either of the two cubes?

The volume of an irregularly shaped object is difficult to determine from a measurement of its dimensions. You can find its volume by the displacement of water, as described in Chapter 1. Use this method to find the density of an irregularly shaped stone. Compare the density of your stone with the results of other students who used pieces that came from the same rock.

- What possible reasons can you give for the different measured values of density of the stones?

11. A block of magnesium whose volume is 10.0 cm³ has a mass of 17.0 g. What is the density of magnesium?

12. a. A 10.0-cm³ block of silver has a mass of 105 g. What is the density of silver?
    b. A 5.0-cm³ block of rock salt has a mass of 10.7 g. What is the density of rock salt?
    c. A sample of alcohol amounting to 0.50 cm³ has a mass of 0.41 g. What is its density?

13. What measurements and what calculations would you make to find the density of the wood in a rectangular block?

14. A student announced that she had made a sample of a new material that had a density of 0.85 g/cm³. Can you tell how large a sample she had made? How?

15. Two cubes of the same size are made of iron and aluminum. How many times as heavy as the aluminum cube is the iron cube? (See Table 3.1, page 52.)

EXPERIMENT

3.6 The Density of Liquids

Examine two samples of liquid. Smell them and shake them, but don't taste them. Can you tell whether they are the same or different? Perhaps by finding their densities, you can answer the question. You can find the density of a liquid by massing it on a balance and measuring its volume with a graduated cylinder. The cylinder is too large to fit easily on the balance. You must mass the liquid in something smaller.

A small amount of liquid will cling to the inside of any container from which you pour it. Therefore, to be certain you mass the volume of the liquid you measure in the graduated cylinder, you must be careful of the order in which you make your measurements of mass and volume.

- Which is more accurate, to mass the liquid in the small container before pouring it into the graduated cylinder, or to determine its volume first?

- What are the densities of the two liquids?

- Are the two liquids the same or different?

16. Suppose you are given two clear, colorless liquids. You measure the densities of these liquids to see whether they are the same substance or different ones.
    a. What would you conclude if you found the densities to be 0.93 g/cm³ and 0.79 g/cm³?
    b. What would you conclude if you found the density of each liquid to be 0.81 g/cm³?

← different substances
← same substance

solutions w/ different concentrations will have different densities but can have the same substance

E X P E R I M E N T

3.7 The Density of a Gas

It is more difficult to measure the density of a gas than that of a liquid or a solid. Gases are hard to handle, and most of them cannot even be seen. In fact, early chemists neglected to take into account the mass of gases produced in experiments.

When we mix Alka-Seltzer tablets and water, a large volume of gas is produced. We can find the density of this gas by massing the tablets and the water before and after they are mixed and by collecting and measuring the volume of the gas. You will recall that, in Experiment 2.6, The Mass of a Gas, you measured the mass of some of this same gas, but you did not measure the volume.

Place two half-tablets of Alka-Seltzer and a test tube with about 5 cm³ of cold water on the pan of your balance as shown in Figure 3.2 (a) or Figure 3.2 (b). Find the total mass of these objects.

Figure 3.2(a)

A good way of supporting the test tube on an electronic balance.

Figure 3.2(b)

A good way of supporting the test tube on a multibeam balance.

Figure 3.3

When the two half-tablets are added to the test tube, the gas generated is collected by displacing water from the inverted bottle on the right.

water in water bottle

do not empty the Test tube until the experiment is totally done or approved

Arrange the apparatus as shown in Figure 3.3 so that you can collect the gas that will be produced. Be sure that the end of the rubber tube is at the top of the collecting bottle and that the whole length of the tube is clear and open.

> **! CAUTION: Always wear safety glasses when you work with gases.**

Drop the two half-tablets into the water, quickly insert the delivery tube and stopper into the test tube, and collect the gas produced. Practically all the gas will be produced in the first ten minutes of the reaction. At the end of this time, remove the delivery tube from the container and then remove the stopper from the test tube.

• Why is it important to hold your hand across the mouth of the bottle while removing it from the container?

Turn the bottle upright, and find the volume of the water that has been displaced by gas.

• How is this volume related to the volume of the gas?
• How can you find the mass of the gas?
• What is the density of the gas?
• What assumptions have you made in using this method?

17. Which of the following choices represents the approximate ratio of the density of the gas in Experiment 3.7 to the density of water (1.0 g/cm³)?
    A. 1/1,000
    B. 1/100
    C. 1/10
    D. about 1
    E. 10
    F. 100
    G. 1,000

18. A mixture of two white solids is placed in a test tube, and the mass of the tube and its contents is found to be 33.66 g. The tube is stoppered, and the apparatus is set up to collect any gas produced. When the tube is gently heated, a gas is given off, and its volume is found to be 470 cm³. After the reaction, the mass of the test tube and its contents is found to be 33.16 g.
    a. What is the mass of the gas collected? .50 (g)
    b. What is the density of the gas collected? .0011 g/cm³

19. Experiment 3.7, The Density of a Gas, is repeated with a sample of a different solid. Here are the data obtained:

Mass of solid, test tube, and water before action	35.40 g
Mass of test tube and contents after action	34.87 g
Volume of gas collected	480 cm³

   Could this gas be the same as that which was produced in Experiment 3.7? NO .0018 is too far apart

20. The volume of gas generated by treating 1.0 g of baking soda with 8.8 g of sulfuric acid is 200 cm³. The remaining acid and solid have a mass of 9.4 g. What is the density of the gas that is produced? .0020 g/cm³

21. If the volume of gas in Question 20 is compressed to 50 cm³, what will be the density of the gas now? To what volume must the gas be compressed before it will reach a density of 1.0 g/cm³, a typical density of a liquid? .008
    density: .40

22. The gas whose density you measured in Experiment 3.7 dissolves slightly in water.
    a. How does this affect the volume of the gas you collect?
    b. How does this affect your determination of the density of the gas?

The volume of the gas decreases b/c when it dissolves, it takes up less space.

This means the density of the gas might actually be higher than it really is.

Handwritten calculations (right margin):
33.66
− 33.16
  .50

.50/470

.53 / 480 = .0011

9.8   .40/200
9.4
 .40

.40/50

3.8 The Range of Densities

Table 3.1 lists the densities of various substances. Note that most solids and liquids have a density that is between 0.5 g/cm³ and about 20 g/cm³. The densities of gases are only about 1/1,000 of the densities of solids and liquids.

Is the density of a substance the same under all conditions? Most substances expand when heated, but their mass remains the same. Therefore, the density depends on the temperature, becoming lower as the material expands and increases in volume. The expansion is very small for solids and liquids and has little effect on the density. The situation is quite different for gases, which expand greatly when heated. Moreover, solids and liquids are difficult to compress, but gases are easily compressed, as you probably know from pumping up a bicycle tire. Therefore, when measuring the density of a gas, we have to state the temperature and the pressure at which the density was measured.

[Handwritten margin notes: volume; mass is same; temperature gets lower; they contract; volume decreases; molecues are tightly packed: density increases (gases)]

Table 3.1 Densities of Some Solids, Liquids, and Gases (in g/cm³)

Substance	Density	Substance	Density	
Osmium	22.5	Oak	0.6–0.9	
Platinum	21.4	Lithium	0.53	
Gold	19.3	Liquid helium		
Mercury	13.6	(at −269°C)	0.15	
Lead	11.3	Liquid hydrogen		
Copper	8.9	(at −252°C)	0.07	
Iron	7.8	Carbon dioxide	1.8×10^{-3} *	
Iodine	4.9	Oxygen	1.3×10^{-3}	
Aluminum	2.7	Air	1.2×10^{-3}	At atmospheric
Carbon tetrachloride	1.60	Nitrogen	1.2×10^{-3}	pressure and room
Water	1.00	Helium	1.7×10^{-4}	temperature
Ice	0.92	Hydrogen	8.4×10^{-5}	
Methyl alcohol	0.79	Air (at 20 km elevation)	9×10^{-5}	

* Small numbers less than 1 can, like large numbers, be expressed in powers of 10. For example, we write 0.1 as 10^{-1}, 0.01 as 10^{-2}, 0.001 as 10^{-3}, and so on, using negative numbers as exponents.

If we have a decimal such as 0.002, we can write it first as 2×0.001, and then, in powers-of-10 notation, as 2×10^{-3}.

Another example: $0.00009 = 9 \times 0.00001 = 9 \times 10^{-5}$. The negative exponent of the 10 tells how many places the decimal point must be moved to the left to give the correct value in ordinary notation.

Refer to Table 3.1 on page 52 to answer the questions.

23. The densities in grams per cubic centimeter of various substances are listed below. For each density, tell whether the substance is most likely to be a gas, a liquid, or a solid.

    a. 0.0015   b. 10.0   c. 0.7   d. 1.1   e. 10^{-4}
    gas   *solid*   *liquid*   *liquid*   *gas*   *gas*

24. Suppose you were given a kilogram of lead and a kilogram of oak. Which would have the greater volume? Which would have the greater mass?
    volume: oak
    mass: same

25. Suppose you had 100 cm³ of gold and 100 cm³ of iron. Which would have the greater mass?
    gold   *volume*

26. A small beaker contains 50 cm³ of liquid.   *63*
    a. If the liquid were methyl alcohol, what would be its mass?
    b. If the liquid were water, what would be its mass?   *50*

27. Estimate the mass of air in an otherwise empty room that is the size of your classroom.

mass / volume = .79

mass / 100 = 19.3   mass / 100

volume
volume of air takes up less space b/c molecules are being pushed down
mass increases not a closed system

50 = 1

EXPERIMENT

3.9 Freezing and Melting

If you live in a part of the country where it snows in the winter, you know that a big pile of snow takes longer to melt than a small one. Does this mean that the big pile melts at a higher temperature? Let us see whether the temperature at which a sample of a substance melts or freezes is really a characteristic property of the substance. To do so, we shall measure the freezing temperatures of some substances by using samples of different mass. For convenience, we shall use substances that freeze above room temperature.

Your teacher will distribute test tubes containing different amounts of a solid substance. Immerse the test tube in a water bath. Heat the water until the solid in the test tube is completely melted.

⚠ **CAUTION: Always wear safety glasses when you use a burner.**

Insert a thermometer into the molten substance. Make sure that the solid in the test tube is completely melted before you remove the burner.

For comparison, it may be interesting also to measure the temperature of the water with a second thermometer. (See Figure 3.4.)

While the liquid in the test tube cools, measure and record both temperatures every half-minute. Stirring the liquid and the water with two thermometers will ensure that the temperatures will be the same throughout each substance.

In addition, record the temperature of the molten substance just as it begins to solidify. Continue to take readings every half-minute until the temperature of the substance drops to about 65°C. You can stop the stirring in the test tube when the thermometer is no longer free to move.

⚠ **CAUTION: To prevent breakage, do not remove the thermometer from the test tube.**

- What was the temperature at which the solid first appeared?
- In your table of temperatures and times, do you note any difference in the way the substance and the water cooled?

A better way to display your results is to plot the temperatures as a function of time on graph paper. Draw the graph of the temperatures of the substance and the water using the same axes. Compare your graphs with those of your classmates.

- Do all graphs have a flat section?
- Does the temperature of the flat section depend on the mass of the cooling materials?
- Do you think that all the samples used in the class were of the same substance?

You have now determined the freezing point of a substance by noting the plateau (flat section) in the cooling curve. For some substances the plateau is more easily recognizable than it is for others. Some cooling curves, however, may not have a flat section at all. For example, look at the cooling curve of candle wax shown in Figure 3.5.

Figure 3.4
Apparatus used to obtain data for the cooling curve of a liquid as it cools and freezes. The thermometer in the test tube measures the temperature of the liquid; the one in the beaker measures that of the water bath. Note that the level of the molten solid in the test tube is below the level of the water in the beaker.

The data for this curve were obtained in the same way as in your experiment. The fact that no part of the curve is flat means that candle wax has no freezing point. In other words, there is no temperature at which it changes from liquid to hard solid without continuing to cool down during the process. Similarly, as you warm a piece of candle wax in your hand, it becomes softer and softer. However, there is no temperature at which it changes from hard solid to liquid without continuing to warm up.

It is harder to measure the melting point of a substance than to measure the freezing point. Since we cannot stir a solid, it is necessary to heat it very slowly and evenly until it melts. If we do so, we find that we get a curve with the flat portion at exactly the freezing temperature. A solid melts at the same temperature at which the liquid form of the same substance freezes.

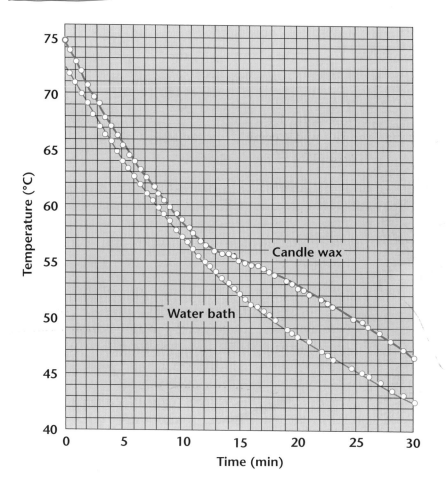

Figure 3.5

The cooling curves of candle wax and of the water bath surrounding the test tube holding the wax. The absence of a flat section in the curve for the wax means that candle wax has no freezing point.

[handwritten margin note:] freezing point: of a substance is a temperature at which a plateau occurs on the cooling curve from liquid to solid

28. The graph in Figure A represents data from an experiment on the cooling of TOP. During which time intervals is there only liquid? only solid? both liquid and solid?

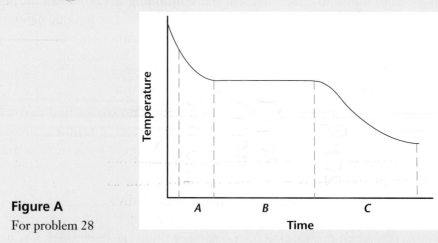

Figure A

For problem 28

29. Water freezes at 0°C. Sketch a graph of temperature as a function of time for a container of water at 20°C, after it is placed in a freezer at –10°C. Show the temperatures +20°C, 0°C, and –10°C on the vertical axis. Continue the graph until practically no further change will take place in the temperature of the ice.

30. A student uses a home freezer in an experiment to find the freezing point of rubbing alcohol. The temperature reaches a plateau at –10°C but the alcohol does not freeze. How can you explain this result?

3.10 Graphing

Drawing graphs effectively is a useful skill. Here are a few guidelines, using Figure 3.5 as an illustration.

The first step in drawing a graph is to set the scales for the horizontal and vertical axes. Let us begin with the horizontal axis. The table of data from which the graphs were made is not given in the text; but we can be quite sure that readings were taken over a period of 30 minutes. Thus, the time axis must cover 30 minutes. If it had covered only 20 minutes, many data points would have been lost. Note that there are 30 divisions on the horizontal axis, so each division corresponds to one minute. This scale makes it easy to locate whole minutes and half-minutes. Looking at the curves, you can recognize which readings were taken at whole minutes and which at half-minutes.

Figure 3.6

The upper left-hand corner of the graph paper in Figure 3.5 with the vertical scale made to extend from 42 to 75 over the 36 divisions. Note how awkward it would be to plot on this scale.

Now look at the vertical axis. The highest temperature reading was close to 75°C, and the lowest reading was close to 42°C. This is a span of 33 C°. Why did the scale not start at 42°C and end at 75°C? Consider the large rectangle to be a sheet of graph paper. It has 36 divisions along the vertical axis. If we had labeled the lower end of the axis as 42°C and the upper end as 75°C, there would have been 33 C° spread over 36 divisions, that is, 33/36 or 0.92 C° per division. It would be very awkward both to plot points and to read their values on such a scale (Figure 3.6). Just try to mark 72.0°C on this scale!

To sum up, the following guidelines will help you choose suitable axes for your graphs:

1. The axes must cover the entire range of your data points.
2. There is no need to start the scale at the smallest value and end it at the largest value.
3. Be sure that each division corresponds to a unit that makes plotting and reading easy.

Once all the points have been plotted, we usually connect them with a smooth curve. Look again at Figure 3.5. Neither of the two curves passes through all the plotted points. Had we drawn the curves through all points, the curves would be full of little wiggles. Because the points stand for measured values, they are subject to uncertainties. In all likelihood the small wiggles are the result of these uncertainties. Therefore, a smooth curve that is close to most points and shows the general trend is a better picture of the results than a curve that goes through all the points. In some cases a curve may not go through any data points.

31. **Suppose a substance was cooled from 83°C to 22°C. Which of the following pairs of temperatures, in Celsius degrees, should you choose for your lowest and highest values on the vertical axis of a graph of the cooling curve?**

A. 0, 100   B. 20, 90   C. 22, 83   D. 30, 80

32. a. What values correspond to points *A* through *D* on scale I of Figure B, and what values correspond to points *E* and *F* on scale II?

  b. Which points are easier to read and why? *scale 1,*

  intervals
  are evenly
  spaced

Figure B

For problem 32

Scale I

2.0   4.5   7   9

A   B   C   D

0   5   10

Scale II

2.5   6.67

E   F

0   5   10

33. On which of the scales shown in Figure C would you choose to plot each of the following sets of numbers? In each case explain the reason for your choice.

  a. 9.0, 17.5, 29.5, 36.0

  b. 17, 23, 55, 62

  c. 23.5, 31.2, 34.8, 39.0

Figure C

For problem 33

I

0   20   40   60   80

II

0   10   20   30   40

III

20   25   30   35   40

34. Examine the horizontal axis on Figure 3.5. What reason can you give for numbering only every 5th division, rather than all the divisions?

EXPERIMENT

3.11 Boiling Point

Everybody knows that it takes longer to bring a full pan of water to a boil than a half-filled one. Does this mean that the full pan gets hotter? To see what happens, heat either 10 cm³ or 20 cm³ of a liquid in a test tube in the apparatus shown in Figure 3.7. To prevent uneven boiling, add a few small chips of porcelain to the liquid. The glass and the rubber tubes will prevent vapors from spreading into the room. The vapors will condense in the cooled test tube.

⚠ CAUTION: Always wear safety glasses when you use a burner.

Some of the liquids you will be using may be flammable. To guarantee gentle heating, use the burner stand as shown in Figure 3.7.

Read the temperature of the liquid every half-minute until the liquid has been boiling for about five minutes. Then plot a graph of the temperature of the liquid as a function of time. Compare your results with those of other students in your class.

- Do all the graphs look alike at the beginning?
- Do all the graphs have a flat section?
- Was the temperature the same in all test tubes once the liquid began boiling?
- What does a difference in boiling point reveal?
- Does the boiling point of a liquid depend on the amount of liquid? Is boiling point a characteristic property?

3.12 Boiling Point and Air Pressure

Suppose your class measured the boiling points of some liquids very carefully and compared the results with those of *IPS* students in schools across the country. You would find that the other schools' results differed slightly from yours. The differences would be greater if the other schools were at different elevations. The boiling point of a liquid depends on the air pressure, which in turn depends on elevation and the weather.

Figure 3.7

A thermometer supported by a rubber stopper in a test tube measures the temperature of a liquid as it is heated to its boiling point. To prevent uneven boiling, a few small chips of porcelain are placed in the liquid. The water in the container should be cold.

liquid to gas

10 A

pressure vapor = atmospheric pressure when boiling begins

boiling point: point where liquid begins to turn a gas

You have changed air pressure many times. Think of a straw in a glass of water. The level of the water inside the straw is the same as the level outside because the air pressure is the same. When you drink through a straw, you remove some of the air, reducing the air pressure in the straw. The difference in pressure causes the water to rise inside the straw until the pressure is again equal.

How high can water rise inside a straw or some other tube? With a long enough tube and a pump to remove the air, the water will rise to a height of about 10 m at sea level. If we replace the water with mercury, the mercury will rise to 0.760 m or 760 mm. This is a much more convenient height to measure (Figure 3.8).

When the top of an evacuated tube containing mercury is sealed and a metric scale is placed next to it, we have a *barometer* (Figure 3.9). The height of the mercury column will show variations. A higher column indicates that the air pushes harder on the surface of the mercury. The height of the column does not depend on the diameter of the tube. This is why the height of the mercury column is used as a measure for the air pressure generated by the atmosphere. This pressure is called *barometric pressure*. In weather reports, barometric pressure is often expressed in inches of mercury.

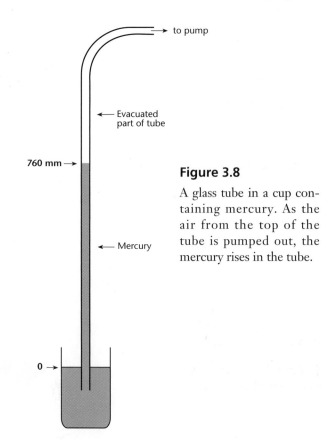

Figure 3.8

A glass tube in a cup containing mercury. As the air from the top of the tube is pumped out, the mercury rises in the tube.

Figure 3.9

The upper and lower parts of a mercury barometer. The long middle section is not shown. The scale on the upper part is in both millimeters and inches. Note that the mercury container at the bottom is much wider than the long tube.

When the barometric pressure is higher, the boiling point of a liquid is higher; when the pressure is lower, the boiling point is lower. The variations in barometric pressure at any one location are rather small. The highest and lowest pressures recorded in Boston, Massachusetts, during one year were 780 and 730 mm, respectively. At these extreme conditions, the boiling point of water varies by only about ±1°C.

The differences in barometric pressure between places at different elevations can be considerable, resulting in significantly different boiling points. The boiling points of water at different elevations are shown in Figure 3.10.

Figure 3.10

A graph of the boiling point of water as a function of elevation above sea level.

35. The highest capital city in the world is La Paz, Bolivia, with an elevation of about 3,600 m. What is the boiling point of water in La Paz?

36. The elevations of Memphis, Tennessee; Boulder, Colorado; and Los Alamos, New Mexico, are 80 m, 1,630 m, and 2,280 m, respectively. What is the boiling point of water in each of these cities?

37. Figure 3.10 shows how the boiling point of water depends on elevation. Under what conditions is it possible for the boiling point of water to exceed 100°C?

3.13 Identifying Substances

We have looked for properties that can help us to distinguish between substances that appear to be the same. So far we have found three properties that do not depend on how much of a substance we have or on its shape. These properties are melting point, boiling point, and density.

Suppose you measured the melting points of two samples of matter and found them to be the same. If you then measured their boiling points and found that these were also the same, you might suspect that you had two samples of the same substance. You would not expect them to differ in their density or in any other properties. But, as Table 3.2 shows, we cannot depend on two properties alone to distinguish between substances, particularly if the measurements are not highly accurate.

In Group 1 of the table, the substances have the same boiling point and nearly the same melting point. It would be hard to measure these two properties carefully enough to see that they are different substances. However, a measurement of their densities would prove without question that they are different.

In Group 2 the substances have the same density and nearly the same boiling point, but can be told apart by their quite different melting points.

If you compared only their densities, you might conclude that the three substances in Group 3 are the same. If you also measured their melting points, you would probably decide that the second and third substances in this group are the same. If you compared their densities and boiling points but not their melting points, which would you conclude

Table 3.2 Some Substances with Similar Properties			
	Density (g/cm³)	Melting point (°C)	Boiling point (°C)
Group 1			
Methyl acetate	0.93	−98	57
Acetone	0.79	−95	57
Group 2			
Isopropanol	0.79	−89	82
t-Butanol	0.79	26	83
Group 3			
Cycloheptane	0.81	−12	118
n-Butanol	0.81	−90	118
s-Butanol	0.81	−89	100

The names of the substances in this table are not important now, and you do not need to remember them. They are good examples of substances that we cannot tell apart unless we measure all three properties: density, melting point, and boiling point.

are the same? In fact, all three substances in Group 3 are different. That is why they were given different names when first discovered.

There are not very many examples of substances that are nearly the same in two of these three properties and yet differ in the third. It would be even harder to find two substances that have the same density, melting point, and boiling point but differ in some other property. If we can determine density, melting point, and boiling point, we can distinguish between almost all substances.

In many cases, the melting point and the boiling point of a sample of matter can be measured easily in the laboratory. However, some substances have boiling points so high that it is difficult to make them hot enough to boil. For example, table salt boils at 1,413°C. Others have boiling points so low that it is difficult even to make them cold enough to become liquid. The same experimental difficulties come up when we try to determine the melting points of some substances. For example, grain alcohol melts at –117°C.

Suppose you have a sample of a newly made substance. You wish to find out whether it is truly a new substance, different from all others, or a substance already known but made in a new way. If its boiling and melting points are too high or too low to measure easily, you must look for other characteristic properties that might help to distinguish it from similar substances.

38. **Which of the substances listed in Table 3.2 are solids, which are liquids, and which are gases at**
    a. **room temperature (20°C)?**
    b. **50°C?**
    c. **100°C?**

39. **Suppose you use the thermometers in your laboratory to measure the boiling points of two liquids. How far apart must the two measurements be in order for you to be confident that the two liquids are different?**

▶ For Review, Applications, and Extensions

40. **Object A has a mass of 500 g and a density of 5.0 g/cm³; object B has a mass of 650 g and a density of 6.5 g/cm³.**
    a. **Which object will displace the most liquid?**
    b. **Could object A and object B be made of the same substance?**

41. A student uses water displacement to measure the volume of a small aluminum ball and then masses it on a balance. He finds that the sphere displaces 4.5 cm³ of water and that the mass of the sphere is 6.5 g.

    a. What value does the student obtain for the density of aluminum?

    b. How can you use this information to decide whether the sphere is sold or hollow ?

42. How can you distinguish between unlabeled pint cartons of milk and of cream without breaking the seals?

43. A student has several different-size samples of substances C and D. She measures the masses and volumes of these samples and plots the graphs shown in Figure D. Which substance has the greater density? How do you know?

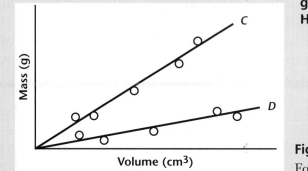

Figure D
For problem 43

44. How can you determine the density of ice? Can you determine the volume of the ice by melting it and measuring the volume of the resulting water? Explain.

45. a. Would adding more ice to an insulated cooler filled with canned drinks make the drinks colder?

    b. If not, how would adding more ice affect the drinks?

    c. Describe an experiment to test your answer to part (b).

46. The melting point of a few tiny crystals of BHT can be measured by placing the crystals in a small capillary tube held next to the bulb of a thermometer in a water bath. (See Figure E). When the melting point is found by this method, the result agrees with the freezing point you found in Experiment 3.9, Freezing and Melting, using about 10 cm³ of the substance.

    a. Use Figure E to estimate the volume of BHT used in the experiment. The inner diameter of the capillary tube is about 0.5 mm.

    b. By what factor is the volume of BHT used in this experiment smaller than that used in Experiment 3.9?

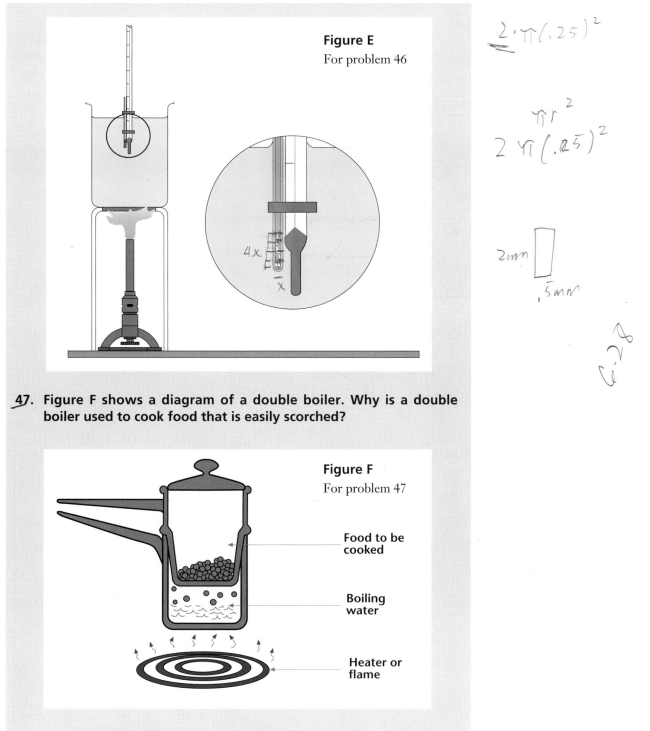

Figure E
For problem 46

$2 \cdot \pi (.25)^2$

πr^2

$2 \pi (.25)^2$

2mm

.5mm

.28

47. Figure F shows a diagram of a double boiler. Why is a double boiler used to cook food that is easily scorched?

Figure F
For problem 47

Food to be cooked

Boiling water

Heater or flame

48. In Table 3.1 on page 52, why are the pressure and temperature stated for the densities of gases and not stated for the densities of solids and liquids?

49. A cylinder is closed with a tight-fitting piston located 30 cm from the end wall (Figure G). The cylinder contains a gas with a density of 1.2×10^{-3} g/cm^3. The piston is pushed in until it is 10 cm from the end wall. If no gas escapes, what is the density of the compressed gas? What is your reasoning?

← 10 cm →

30 cm

Figure G

For problem 49

50. Does the density of air change when it is heated
    a. in an open bottle?
    b. in a tightly stoppered bottle?

THEMES FOR SHORT ESSAYS

1. Ice floats on water. Suppose it did not. What would happen to life in lakes and rivers? Write a short science-fiction story on this subject.

2. Write a short mystery story in which a criminal tries to pass off a small statue of gold-plated lead as solid gold. Have the detective uncover the plot without damaging the statue.

4 Solubility

EXPERIMENT

4.1 Dissolving a Solid in Water

You know from daily experience that sand and chalk do not dissolve in water, but that sugar and table salt do. Of course, these are only qualitative observations—that is, observations that do not involve measurement. Are you sure that not even a tiny amount of chalk or sand dissolves in a gallon of water? Can you dissolve as much salt or sugar as you wish in a glass of water?

Many solutions are colorless—there is nothing to be seen once the solid is dissolved. To make things visible, we shall begin our quantitative study of solutions with a solution that has color.

Place 5.0 cm³ of water in one test tube and 20.0 cm³ of water in another. Add 0.30 g of orange solid (or 0.15 g of blue solid) to each tube, then stopper and shake thoroughly.

> ⚠ **CAUTION: Be careful not to get any solution on your hands. If some spills, wash thoroughly with water.**

- Did all of the solid dissolve in both test tubes?
- Do you think that each cubic centimeter of solution contains the same mass of dissolved material?
- Both tubes contain the same mass of dissolved material, but is the shade of the color the same in both tubes?
- Will another 0.30 g of the orange solid (or 0.15 g of the blue solid) dissolve in each of the test tubes? Try it, but be patient!

The solution may cool as the solid dissolves. If so, try to keep the temperature fairly constant by warming the test tube with your hand.

- Did 0.60 g of the orange solid (or 0.30 g of the blue solid) dissolve as well in 20.0 cm³ as in 5.0 cm³ of water?
- Is the color uniform in each solution?
- Is the shade of the color the same in both solutions?

Add another 0.30 g of the orange solid (or 0.15 g of the blue solid) to each solution.

- How much do you have in each test tube?
- What do you observe?
- How much orange (or blue) solid do you think there would have to be in the 20.0-cm³ test tube before the solid stopped dissolving? Test your prediction.

A solution in which no more solid can be dissolved is called a *saturated solution*.

> 1. Some people say that sugar "melts" when it is added to water. How would you describe the difference between melting and dissolving?

4.2 Concentration

In the last experiment, the color changed as you added more solid, but the color was uniform throughout each test tube. This uniformity of color suggests that the solid dissolved uniformly. That is, a cubic centimeter of water in a given solution contained the same mass of orange (or blue) material as any other cubic centimeter of water in that solution. For example, if you used the orange solid, at the beginning of the experiment one test tube contained

$$\frac{0.30 \text{ g}}{5.0 \text{ cm}^3} = 0.060 \text{ g/cm}^3$$

of material and the other test tube contained

$$\frac{0.30 \text{ g}}{20.0 \text{ cm}^3} = 0.015 \text{ g/cm}^3$$

The mass of solid dissolved per unit volume of liquid is called the *concentration* of the solution. The unit of concentration is the same as that of density, g/cm^3. However, in the case of density, the mass and the volume refer to the same substance. In the case of concentration, the mass refers to the dissolved solid (called the *solute*) and the volume refers to the liquid (called the *solvent*).

To avoid confusion and for convenience, concentrations are often given in $g/100 \text{ cm}^3$. For example, a concentration of 0.015 g/cm^3 means that 0.015 g of solute is dissolved in 1 cm^3 of water. Hence, a volume of 100 cm^3 of water will contain

$$100 \times 0.015 \text{ g} = 1.5 \text{ g}$$

of solute. Thus, the concentration of the solution given in $g/100 \text{ cm}^3$ is $1.5 \text{ g}/100 \text{ cm}^3$. In general, to express the concentration of a solution in $g/100 \text{ cm}^3$, multiply the concentration in g/cm^3 by 100.

2. A mass of 25.0 g of sugar is dissolved in 150 cm³ of water. What is the concentration in
   a. g/cm³?
   b. g/10 cm³?
   c. g/100 cm³?

   $$\frac{25}{150}$$

3. Which solution is more concentrated, 2.5 g/cm³ or 2.6 g/10 cm³?

4. Which of the following steps will increase the concentration of a solution of salt and water?
   A. Allowing some of the water to evaporate
   B. Adding water to the solution
   C. Adding salt to the solution
   D. Pouring out some of the solution

5. For Experiment 4.1, Dissolving a Solid in Water, calculate the concentration of the solutions in g/cm³ and in g/100 cm³ after the addition of each sample of solid.

6. What was the greatest concentration you were able to achieve in Experiment 4.1, Dissolving a Solid in Water?

EXPERIMENT

4.3 Comparing the Concentrations of Saturated Solutions

From the results of dissolving the orange or blue solid (Experiment 4.1, Dissolving a Solid in Water), you know that there is a point at which no more solute will dissolve in the solvent. The solution then has the largest possible concentration and is called a saturated solution, as stated in Section 4.1.

To find the concentration of a saturated solution, you could add the solid a tiny amount at a time and see whether it dissolves. A better method is to add a large mass of solid to a solvent and shake the container until you judge that no more solid will dissolve. Then you can pour off some of the clear liquid and find the concentration.

Try dissolving 5 g of two solids in separate test tubes, each containing 5 cm³ of water. Stopper the test tubes, and shake them vigorously for several minutes until the solution is saturated. If the tube cools during the process, keep it warm with your hand.

• Does one sample of solid appear to be more soluble in water than the other?

④ To find the concentrations of the two saturated solutions, you can evaporate the liquid from a known mass of each solution. Subtracting the mass of the remaining dry solid from the mass of the solution will give you the mass and, therefore, the volume of the water in your sample. This will give you the data you need to calculate the concentration of the saturated solution. You can do the experiment for one solution while some of your classmates work with the other solution.

⑤ Pour almost all the saturated solution into a previously massed evaporating dish. Be careful not to pour out so much solution that undissolved solid is carried over from the test tube into the dish.

⑥ After finding the total mass of dish and solution, slowly evaporate the saturated solution to dryness over a flame, as shown in Figure 4.1, and ⑦ find the mass of the remaining solid.

⚠ **CAUTION: Always wear safety glasses when you use a burner.**

Be careful to heat the solution very slowly so that solid does not spatter out of the dish. Keep watching the dish, and move the flame away whenever spattering begins.

- What is the mass of the solid and the mass of the water in which it dissolved?
- What is the volume of the water?
- What is the concentration of each of the saturated solutions?
- How would the calculated concentration be affected if some of the undissolved solid had carried over from the test tube to the dish?
- How do your results compare with those of your classmates?

The concentration of a saturated solution is called the _solubility_. In this experiment you found the solubilities of two substances in the same solvent, namely water.

Solubility is independent of the mass of the sample from which it is found. It is a characteristic property of the combination of the solute and the solvent.

Figure 4.1

Evaporating a solution in an evaporating dish heated over a microburner. If the liquid spatters, it should be heated more slowly by moving the burner to one side so that the flame heats only one edge of the dish.

7. Suppose you dissolve 0.60 g of a powder in 20.0 cm³ of water. The solution is not saturated. Which of the following outcomes might be observed if the solution was left in an open dish for several days?

   A. Some water evaporated and there is no solid at the bottom of the dish.

   B. Some water evaporated and there is some solid at the bottom of the dish.

   C. Only solid remains in the dish.

8. A student poured 60 g of sodium nitrate into 100 cm³ of water and observed that all the solid dissolved. Which of the following can she conclude about the solubility of sodium nitrate in water?

   A. It is less than 60 g/100 cm³.

   B. It is 60 g/100 cm³.

   C. It is greater than 60 g/100 cm³.

9. A solid is placed in a container with water and stirred thoroughly. Some solid dissolves and some remains at the bottom of the container.

   a. Will adding more water and stirring cause more of the solid to dissolve?

   b. Does adding more water increase the solubility of the solid?

10. Mario wishes to construct a table that lists the solubility in water of several substances. From various sources, he finds the following data for solubilities at 0°C.

    a. Boric acid   0.20 g in 10 cm³ of water
    b. Bromine   25 g in 600 cm³ of water
    c. Washing soda   220 g in 1,000 cm³ of water
    d. Baking soda   24 g in 350 cm³ of water

    Find the solubility of each substance in g/100 cm³ of water.

11. From your answers to Question 10, find the largest mass of each substance that will dissolve in 60 cm³ of water.

12. Suppose that 200 cm³ of a saturated solution of potassium nitrate were left standing in an open beaker on your laboratory desk for three weeks. During this time most of the water evaporated.

    a. Would the mass of potassium nitrate dissolved in the solution change?

    b. Would the concentration of the potassium nitrate solution change during the three weeks?

EXPERIMENT

4.4 The Effect of Temperature on Solubility

In the last experiment, you tried to keep the temperature of the solution constant (by warming the test tube with your hand if it cooled). How are the solubilities of different substances affected by the temperature of the liquid? Remember that solubility is the maximum mass of a solid that will dissolve in a given volume of liquid.

To find out, add 10 g of two solids to two test tubes, each of which contains 10 cm³ of water. Place both test tubes in a large beaker of water, and stir the solutions for several minutes until they are saturated. Now heat the beaker, stirring both solutions constantly, until the water in the beaker is near boiling.

> ⚠ **CAUTION: Always wear safety glasses when you use a burner.**

- What do you observe?
- Do the solubilities of the substances appear to change equally or differently as the temperature of the water is increased?
- What do you predict will happen if you remove the burner and cool both test tubes together in a beaker of cold water? Try it.

Figure 4.2 shows the result of an experiment with potassium sulfate. The solubility at different temperatures was measured by the same

Figure 4.2
A graph of the solubility of potassium sulfate as a function of temperature. Note that the line does not extend through all the points (Section 3.10).

method you used in Experiment 4.3, Comparing the Concentrations of Saturated Solutions. The solubility is expressed as the mass in grams of the substance that is dissolved in 100 cm³ of water to give a saturated solution or, to put it another way, the maximum mass of the substance that can be dissolved in 100 cm³ of water.

Suppose we first dissolve 20 g of potassium sulfate in 100 cm³ of water at 80°C, and then cool the solution to room temperature, or 20°C. Figure 4.2 shows that the water can hold only 12 g of potassium sulfate in solution at this temperature. Therefore, at about 70°C, small crystals of solid potassium sulfate begin to appear in the solution during the cooling process. As cooling continues, more crystals are produced in the solution, and they sink to the bottom. A solid that crystallizes out of a saturated solution in this manner is called a *precipitate*. In this case, the mass of potassium sulfate that will precipitate out of solution and collect at the bottom will be 20 g – 12 g = 8 g.

Figure 4.3

Solubility curves of different substances in water as a function of temperature.

Figure 4.3 shows solubility as a function of temperature for several common substances, all plotted together on the same graph. These curves clearly show that the way the solubility of a substance changes with temperature is a characteristic property that can help to distinguish between different substances. You can see from the graph, for example, that the solubilities of potassium nitrate and sodium chloride (ordinary table salt) are very nearly the same at room temperature (about 20°C) but are widely different at high and low temperatures.

[handwritten margin: solubility vs temp]

[handwritten margin sketch and notes: always the were volume talking about]

13. **Examine Figure 4.3. At what temperature are the solubilities of potassium nitrate and sodium chloride equal?** *25°*

14. **How many grams of sodium chloride can be dissolved in 100 cm³ of water at room temperature (about 20°C)? at 100°C?** *① 35° ② 40°*

15. **Suppose you have a saturated solution of potassium sulfate at room temperature. From Figure 4.2, what do you predict will happen if you**
   a. **heat the solution?** *the solubility will increase [dissolve]*
   b. **cool the solution?** *precipitation*

16. **If you plotted the data from Figure 4.2 on Figure 4.3, where would the curve be found?**

17. **Give a reason for heating the solutions in Experiment 4.4, The Effect of Temperature on Solubility, by immersing the test tubes in a beaker of hot water rather than heating the test tubes directly over a burner flame.** *the solutions would heat more evenly & be distributed so we can get an accurate result*

18. **What temperature is required to dissolve 110 g of sodium nitrate in 100 cm³ of water?** *47°*

19. a. **If 20 g of sodium chloride is dissolved in 100 cm³ of water at 20°C, is the solution saturated?** *NO*
   b. **How can you determine whether a solution is saturated?** *If a point [part of the line] is on the point our solubility of sodium chloride starts at 35*

20. **A mass of 30 g of potassium nitrate is dissolved in 100 cm³ of water at 20°C. The solution is heated to 100°C. How many more grams of potassium nitrate must be added to saturate the solution?** *30/100 212 g.*

21. **A mass of 10 g of sodium nitrate is dissolved in 10 cm³ of water at 80°C. As the solution is cooled, at what temperature will a precipitate first appear?**

10 × 10 = 100 g
10 × 10 = 100 cm³ } b/c graph is in 100 cm³
140°C

[handwritten margin: x g 150° 100°C   3.0 g 15 20°C   242   30   212   (20)]

4.5 Wood Alcohol and Grain Alcohol

Most rocks and metals, and many other materials, are so slightly soluble in water that we cannot measure the very small amounts that dissolve. Water, however, is not the only liquid. Perhaps some substances that hardly dissolve at all in water will dissolve easily in other liquids. If so, we can use the different solubilities of substances in these liquids to distinguish between them, as we did with materials soluble in water. We shall first consider wood alcohol and grain alcohol, two common liquids. Then we shall see if there are other solvents that will further increase our stock of tools for investigating matter.

Wood alcohol, as its name implies, was first made from wood. The ancient Syrians heated wood in order to obtain the liquids and tars that resulted. The watery liquids (including the alcohol) were used as solvents and as fuel for lamps. The tars were used to fill the seams in boats, to preserve wood against rot, and as mortar for bricks.

The method used by the Syrians in making these substances was quite crude. Lengths of wood were stacked closely in a dishlike depression in the top of a mound of earth. A drain ran from the middle of the depression to a collection pit. After the wood was covered with green branches and wet leaves, a fire was started inside the pile. As this fire smoldered, watery liquids and tars drained off from the pile and collected in the pit. Later it was discovered that the watery liquids could be separated. One of these liquids was wood alcohol.

Grain alcohol can be made by fermenting grains, such as corn, barley, and rye, as well as by fermenting grapes and other fruits. Fermentation is the process that goes on naturally when fruit juice or damp grain is stored with little exposure to air. Gas bubbles out of the liquid, and what remains boils at a temperature lower than the boiling point of water. As had been discovered long before the beginning of recorded history, this liquid contains a new substance, different from water, which was used as a beverage and as a medicine.

By the twelfth century, the wine from fermented grapes was boiled and the vapor collected and allowed to cool. The condensed liquid was described as the "water that burns." It was named *alcohol vini*, or "essence of wine," and later came to be called grain alcohol.

If you measure the densities of the alcohols from different grains and fruits, you find no difference between them. These alcohols also have the same boiling point and melting (or freezing) point. In fact, they are all the same substance. Similarly, the alcohols (or essences) produced from different kinds of wood are all the same: all have the same density, boiling point, and melting point. Since the liquids obtained from wood and fermented grain are both called alcohol, you might think that they are the same substance. But from an examination of Table 4.1, you see that they are indeed different. Though their densities are nearly the same, their melting points and boiling points differ enough so that there can be no possibility that they are the same substance. Today, wood alcohol is called *methanol*, and grain alcohol is called *ethanol*.

Table 4.1 Some Characteristic Properties of the Most Common Alcohols			
	Density (g/cm³)	Melting point (°C)	Boiling point (°C)
Wood alcohol (methanol)	0.79	−94	65
Grain alcohol (ethanol)	0.79	−117	79

Ethanol is the important ingredient in alcoholic beverages. Methanol, on the other hand, is very poisonous. Some methanol, or other poison, is usually added to ethanol to make burner fuel undrinkable. Ethanol treated this way is said to be "denatured." Ethanol is now also added to gasoline in some parts of the United States to reduce the consumption of gasoline.

Both of these alcohols will dissolve many substances that are insoluble in water, and both have been used for centuries as solvents. During the nineteenth century, substances with properties similar to those of methanol and ethanol were made in the laboratory. They were also called alcohols. A common alcohol is *isopropanol*, also known as rubbing alcohol. Isopropanol also dissolves many substances insoluble in water. You will use isopropanol in the next experiment.

EXPERIMENT

4.6 Isopropanol as a Solvent

Sugar and citric acid look the same. They are both white. Their densities are so close that you could not distinguish between them with the equipment used in this course. Their solubility in water is also not much help because both substances are very soluble in water.

Suggest a way to distinguish between these two substances by using their solubility in isopropanol. Have your teacher approve your plan before you begin.

⚠ **CAUTION: Do not inhale isopropanol vapor.**

- How do the solubilities of sugar and citric acid in isopropanol help to distinguish between these substances?

You can also test the solubilities of other substances, such as TOP and baking soda.

- Does TOP dissolve in water? in isopropanol?
- Does baking soda dissolve in water? in isopropanol?

You can see how valuable solubility in different solvents is for distinguishing between substances. Suppose you have samples of two solids that look alike and dissolve about equally well in one solvent but very differently in a second solvent. You can be certain that the two solids are different substances. You saw an example of this in the case of sugar and citric acid in isopropanol.

Likewise, two similar liquids can be distinguished if a substance dissolves to a much greater extent in one liquid than in the other. You saw examples of this in the case of the solubility of TOP or sugar in water and isopropanol.

Solubility is another characteristic property of a substance, a tool that you can add to your list of ways to distinguish between substances. With the addition of solubility, you do not always have to measure the density, melting point, or boiling point to distinguish between substances. The more tools you have for distinguishing between substances, the easier your job becomes.

22. a. Which of the following substances, X, Y, and Z, do you think are the same? X ₃ Y
    b. How might you test them further to make sure? Find solubility in different solvent

Substance	Density (g/cm³)	Melting point (°C)	Boiling point (°C)	Solubility in water at 20°C (g/100 cm³)	Solubility in methanol at 20°C
X	1.63	80	327	20	insoluble
Y	1.63	81	326	19	insoluble
Z	1.62	60	310	156	insoluble

EXPERIMENT

4.7 The Solubility of Carbon Dioxide

The gas you produced by heating baking soda in Experiment 1.1, and whose density you measured in Experiment 3.7, is called *carbon dioxide*. It is a part of the air you exhale at every breath.

Carbon dioxide is produced by a variety of substances when they burn, including wood and gasoline. Since carbon dioxide does not burn, it makes a good fire extinguisher. With a density greater than air, it simply smothers the fire like a blanket.

Is carbon dioxide soluble in water? Figure 4.4 shows the equipment you will use to generate carbon dioxide gas and to collect it by water displacement.

> ⚠ **CAUTION: Always wear safety glasses when you work with gases.**

Before you begin to generate the gas, you need to prepare the known volume of water in which you are going to dissolve it. An easy way of doing this is to fill completely the collecting bottle with cold tap water

Figure 4.4

Equipment used to collect a full bottle of carbon dioxide and to measure its solubility. The large test tube contains 10 cm^3 of water and the inverted collecting bottle is filled with water. The volume of water in the container on the right is the same as the volume of the collecting bottle.

and pour it into the container in which you will later invert the collecting bottle. This container is shown on the right in Figure 4.4. To find the volume of the collecting bottle, you can use your 250-mL beaker that has graduation marks.

- What is the volume of the collecting bottle?

Two Alka-Seltzer tablets (four halves) placed in the test tube will generate enough gas to fill the collecting bottle. After adding the tablets, quickly put the rubber stopper in place and carefully insert the delivery tube into the top of the collecting bottle. While you do this, the carbon dioxide will force the air out of the test tube and the rubber tube so it will not be collected.

- How will you know when you have collected a full bottle of carbon dioxide?

When the collecting bottle is completely filled with gas, invert it in the container having the same volume of water (Figure 4.5). Be sure not to lose any gas in the process.

Gases, like most substances, do not dissolve rapidly. Try moving the inverted plastic bottle back and forth in the larger container in order to cause a little water to enter its mouth. Be careful to keep the mouth of the bottle against the bottom of the container so that no bubbles of carbon dioxide escape. As more gas dissolves and water rises into the collecting bottle, you can shake it back and forth more and more vigorously. The shaking also mixes the water inside and outside the collecting bottle, ensuring that the gas is dissolved in all the water.

- After 10 to 15 minutes of shaking, does the carbon dioxide continue to dissolve?

- How will you know when the water has become saturated with carbon dioxide?

Figure 4.5

A bottle full of gas ready to be placed in the container of water. To prevent the gas from escaping, be sure to hold your hand over the mouth of the bottle until it is under water. (Blue coloring was added to the water for contrast.)

Figure 4.6

A bottle full of gas placed in the container of water. Shake the inverted bottle back and forth vigorously so that the gas and water mix well. Hold the mouth of the bottle firmly against the bottom of the plastic container to prevent any gas from escaping. (Blue color was added to the water for contrast.)

In order to measure the volume of gas that dissolved, the bottle must be turned upright without losing any saturated solution from inside it. This can be done by quickly inverting the entire assembly shown in Figure 4.6 over a large sink. Only the solution from the container that is outside the bottle will spill into the sink.

- When the water becomes saturated, what is the volume of carbon dioxide gas that does not dissolve?
- What is the volume of carbon dioxide that does dissolve?
- Use the class data of Experiment 3.7, The Density of a Gas, to find the mass of carbon dioxide that dissolved in the saturated solution.
- What is the volume of water in the saturated solution?
- What is the solubility of carbon dioxide in g/100 cm³ of water?

23. **When conducting Experiment 4.7, a student stopped shaking the inverted bottle before all the carbon dioxide had completely dissolved. How does this affect the calculated solubility of the gas?**

24. **Suppose the water rose to completely fill the inverted collecting bottle used in Experiment 4.7. How would this affect the calculated solubility of carbon dioxide? Explain your reasoning.**

25. **Suppose Experiment 3.7, The Density of a Gas, was done twice, but with one tablet and 15 cm³ of water in each case. When the rubber tube was placed as shown in Figure 3.3, 435 cm³ of gas was collected. When the tube reached only slightly beyond the mouth of the bottle, only 370 cm³ of gas was collected. The change in mass of the reactants was the same in both cases.**
    a. **What volume of gas dissolved in the water?**
    b. **Use the class data of Experiment 3.7 to find what mass of gas dissolved in the water.**

4.8 The Solubility of Gases

Table 4.2 shows the solubilities of several gases in water. It is clear from the table that the solubility of gases varies greatly. Gases of low solubility can be collected by water displacement. Others, such as hydrogen chloride, cannot be collected over water. Hydrogen chloride was prepared over two hundred years ago by the French chemist Antoine Lavoisier by reacting sulfuric acid with table salt. He collected the gas by displacement of mercury.

Table 4.2 The Solubility of Gases in Water at Various Temperatures (in g/100 cm³)

Temperature (°C)	Nitrogen	Oxygen	Carbon dioxide	Sulfur dioxide	Hydrogen chloride	Ammonia
0	2.4×10^{-3}	7.0×10^{-3}	0.34	23	82	90
20	1.9×10^{-3}	4.4×10^{-3}	0.17	11	72	53
40	1.4×10^{-3}	3.3×10^{-3}	0.10	5.5	63	32
60	1.1×10^{-3}	2.8×10^{-3}	0.07	3.3	56	14

You can see in Table 4.2 that the solubility of nitrogen is small compared with those of hydrogen chloride and ammonia, which are two of the most soluble gases known. The solubility of all the gases in Table 4.2 decreases as the temperature increases. This behavior is different from that of solids, which you observed in Experiment 4.4, The Effect of Temperature on Solubility, and in Figures 4.2 and 4.3. The solubility of most solids increases with temperature but that of most gases diminishes.

26. Look at Table 4.2. Which gas is the most soluble at 0°C? at 60°C?

27. From the data in Table 4.2, draw a graph of the solubilities of hydrogen chloride and ammonia versus temperature. At what temperature do the two gases have the same solubility in water?

28. Fish prefer to live in cool water that has splashed over rocks rather than in warm water that is stagnant. Based upon information in Table 4.2, present an explanation for this observation.

29. A collection bottle contains 500 cm³ of ammonia.
    a. The density of ammonia is 7.7×10^{-4} g/100 cm³ at atmospheric pressure and room temperature. What is the mass of ammonia in the bottle?

 b. What do expect to happen when the bottle is inverted and placed in a container having 1,000 cm³ of water?

30. Carbonated soft drinks can be transported in the sun and stored at room temperature. When they are opened cool, they fizz, showing that the solution is saturated in carbon dioxide.
 a. What do you think happens to the carbon dioxide in the water when the bottles are in the sun?
 b. Why do glass bottles containing carbonated drinks sometimes explode when left in the sun for too long?
 c. What happens to the carbon dioxide when the bottles cool down again?

4.9 Acid Rain

When some gases, such as carbon dioxide, sulfur dioxide, and hydrogen chloride, are dissolved in water, the properties of the solution are very different from those of water alone. These solutions have a sour taste and are able to dissolve minerals and metals to a much greater extent than water. They are called *acidic solutions*.

 Raindrops dissolve carbon dioxide as they pass through the atmosphere, forming an acidic solution known as *carbonic acid*. Limestone and chalk are much more soluble in carbonic acid than in water. When rains seep through the soil over a long time, a very large volume of acidic water can come into contact with limestone rock below the surface. This large volume of water can dissolve a large amount of limestone, leaving an empty space beneath the soil's surface. When the soil above this empty space can no longer support itself, it collapses, as shown in Figure 4.7.

Figure 4.7

A "sinkhole" in central Florida. Limestone below the top layer was dissolved in water containing much carbon dioxide. (*AP/Wide World Photos*)

Figure 4.8

A statue of Civil-War General William F. Draper in Milford, Massachusetts. The statue, made in 1912 and photographed in 1987, has been damaged by acid rain. *(Courtesy, Center for Conservation and Technical Studies, Harvard University Art Museums)*

Figure 4.9

Spruce trees on White Face Mountain in New York that have been killed by acid rain. *(USDA Forest Service)*

Carbon dioxide is produced and added to the atmosphere when coal, oil, wood, and gasoline are burned. Consumption of these fuels is increasing worldwide. Thus, the concentration of carbon dioxide in the atmosphere is increasing.

Much of the coal that we burn as fuel contains sulfur. When sulfur is burned, sulfur dioxide is produced. As you can see in Table 4.2, sulfur dioxide has a higher solubility in water than does carbon dioxide. Water falling to the earth that contains dissolved sulfur dioxide is called *acid rain*.

Acid rain dissolves the surface of stone used in buildings and statues, as shown in Figure 4.8. It can also damage or kill plants, as Figure 4.9 shows. If enough acid rain or snow accumulates in lakes and ponds, it is harmful to the animals living there.

4.10 Drinking Water

Most people get their drinking water from wells, rivers, or lakes. This water was once rain or snow that travelled great distances through the air, over rocks and land, and through soil, dissolving many substances along the way. In addition to dissolved minerals, drinking water may contain fertilizers, herbicides, pesticides, and other substances made by people.

The concentrations of substances dissolved in drinking water are very low. If they were not, the water would be harmful and have a strange taste. As an example, the concentration of ordinary table salt in your water is probably below 0.005 g/100 cm^3. The concentrations of several substances in the drinking water of three cities are listed in Table 4.3.

The concentrations listed in Table 4.3 are very low compared with the solubilities that you measured and observed in earlier sections. Also, the concentrations listed vary from substance to substance and city to city.

Table 4.3 Analysis of City Water Supplies

Substance	Concentration (g/100 cm³)		
	Belmont, MA	Denver, CO	Memphis, TN
Arsenic chloride	$< 2.4 \times 10^{-6}$	$< 2.4 \times 10^{-6}$	$< 1.2 \times 10^{-6}$
Calcium carbonate	1.2×10^{-3}	2.2×10^{-3}	1.2×10^{-3}
Iron chloride	1.4×10^{-6}	1.4×10^{-5}	9.6×10^{-5}
Lead nitrate	$< 2.8 \times 10^{-7}$	$< 2.8 \times 10^{-7}$	1.4×10^{-7}
Mercury chloride	$< 2.7 \times 10^{-8}$	$< 1.4 \times 10^{-8}$	$< 2.7 \times 10^{-8}$
Sodium chloride	2.0×10^{-3}	5.1×10^{-3}	2.5×10^{-3}
Potassium nitrate	2.6×10^{-4}	1.8×10^{-4}	1.8×10^{-4}

Sodium chloride, iron chloride, and calcium carbonate are examples of substances that are not very toxic but affect the taste of water. Water that contains too much iron has a strange taste and leaves a rust-colored stain in containers. Water containing excessive amounts of calcium carbonate is said to be *hard water*. This water has a mineral-like taste and soaps do not lather or clean effectively in it.

Other substances are important because small concentrations of them in drinking water can be dangerous to people's health. Substances that contain arsenic, lead, and mercury are toxic substances that are harmful if present in too high a concentration in drinking water.

If too much acid rain becomes a part of the water supply, drinking water becomes able to dissolve metals. When acidic drinking water passes through lead pipes or pipes having joints sealed with lead solder, some of this lead dissolves in the drinking water.

Drinking water with a high enough concentration of lead can cause damage to the brain and other parts of the nervous system. Lead seems to affect young children more than adults. Perhaps this is because lead is not eliminated from the body quickly, as many other toxic substances are. Instead, it accumulates in the body, so that its concentration increases as time passes.

31. Which city listed in Table 4.3 has the hardest water?

32. A typical person drinks about two liters (2,000 cm³) of water a day. How much sodium chloride would a person in Memphis take in from drinking water each day? How much in a year?

33. Why would it be unwise to pass a law stating that if any toxic substances were shown to be in a municipality's drinking water, the water could not be distributed and used by its citizens?

34. Large deposits of sodium chloride or potassium nitrate near the surface of the earth are found mostly in deserts. Why?

▶ For Review, Applications, and Extensions

35. Each of four test tubes contains 10 cm³ of water at 25°C. The following masses of an unknown solid are placed in the test tubes: 4 g in the first, 8 g in the second, 12 g in the third, and 16 g in the fourth. After the tubes are shaken, all of the solid has dissolved in the first two tubes, but some undissolved solid remains in the other two tubes.
    a. What is the concentration of the solid in each of the first two tubes?
    b. What can you say about the concentration of the solid in the second two tubes?

36. a. Which of the substances shown in Figure 4.3 could be the unknown solid of Question 35?
    b. If the unknown is indeed the substance you named in answer to part (a), what will happen if the solution in each test tube is cooled to 10°C?

37. The solubility of a substance in water at various temperatures is shown below. What would you expect the solubility to be at 60°C? at 100°C? Explain.

Temperature (°C)	Solubility (g/100 cm³)
25	5
50	10
75	15

38. In many localities, after a kettle has been used for some time for boiling water, a flaky solid appears on the inside-bottom and on the sides of the kettle that have been in contact with the water. How do you account for the presence of this "boiler scale"?

39. There are two kinds of felt-tip (magic-marker) pens. Some are labeled "permanent" and some are labeled "water color."
    a. What does the label tell you about the solubility in water of the dye in the two inks?
    b. Do you think the liquid in both inks is water?

40. In dry cleaning, a garment is sprayed with liquids that dissolve various stains. Often a brightly colored cotton shirt carries a label: "Dry clean only—colors may bleed when washed."
    a. What does such a label tell you about the solubility of the dye in hot water containing a detergent or soap?
    b. Do you think the dye dissolves in cold tap water?

41. An Alka-Seltzer tablet is dissolved in 10 cm³ of water, and the gas is collected as in Experiment 3.7, The Density of a Gas. The volume of gas collected is 450 cm³. When 50 cm³ of water is used, the volume of gas collected is 400 cm³. The tube was all the way up in the bottle in both cases.
    a. Why do you think less gas is collected when more water is used to dissolve the tablet?
    b. Would this make a difference in the density calculation?

42. If you have a certain amount of a solid to dissolve in water, you usually can speed up the process in various ways. Why do you think each of the following steps is effective in making the solid dissolve faster?
    a. Stirring the water
    b. Crushing the solid into smaller particles
    c. Heating the water

43. In Experiment 3.7, The Density of a Gas, you were directed to insert the rubber delivery tube all the way up to the bottom of the inverted collection bottle before collecting any gas. In Experiment 4.7, you began to generate carbon dioxide gas before inserting the delivery tube into the collection bottle. Why was it unnecessary to push the delivery tube up to the bottom of the inverted collection bottle? Explain the significance of the variations between the two procedures.

44. Water analyses usually give the concentrations of dissolved substances in parts per million (ppm). If the concentration of sodium chloride in drinking water was listed as 14 ppm, what would its concentration be in g/100 cm³?

45. The concentration of calcium carbonate in Denver's drinking water is 2.2×10^{-3} g/100 cm³ (Table 4.3). Yet, at 25°C the solubility of calcium carbonate in pure water is only 1.4×10^{-3} g/100 cm³. How can the concentration be higher than the solubility?

Theme for a Short Essay

Write an episode in a mystery centered on the possibility of selectively dissolving some substances mixed in with others. For example, a secret message written in ink may be covered by a painting. Describe real (not fictitious) substances.

5 The Separation of Mixtures

In this chapter we shall use the characteristic properties studied so far to work out a variety of methods for separating mixtures. These mixtures may be gases, liquids, or solids. A mixture of liquids can be separated by boiling the mixture, condensing the vapor, and carefully collecting the resulting liquids. This process is called *fractional distillation*.

EXPERIMENT

5.1 Fractional Distillation

In this experiment you will determine some of the properties of a mixture of liquids. Then you will distill the mixture and examine the properties of the fractions to see if you succeeded in separating the liquids that made up the original mixture.

Part A

- Can you tell just by looking at it that the liquid is a mixture?
- Does the liquid have an odor?

Dip a small piece of paper in the liquid, and with a match try lighting the liquid on the paper.

> ⚠ **CAUTION: Always wear safety glasses when you work with a flame. Put a bucket of water on your table in case the paper burns.**

- Does the liquid burn?
- What is its density?
- Does sugar dissolve in the liquid?

Part B

Use the apparatus shown in Figure 5.1 to distill 5 cm³ of the mixture. Use a single collecting tube and heat the liquid just enough to keep it boiling. Record the temperature of the vapor from the boiling liquid every half-minute while it distills. Continue to boil the liquid almost to dryness.
Make a graph of the temperature of the vapor as a function of time.

- What do you conclude from your graph about the number of fractions you should collect to separate the different substances in the mixture?
- At what temperatures should you shift from one collecting tube to another?

Indicate on your graph the temperatures at which you decided to change collecting tubes.

Figure 5.1

Apparatus for the fractional distillation of a liquid. The thermometer bulb is close to the top of the test tube so that it measures the temperature of the vapor that condenses in the outlet tube. If there is more than one liquid in the boiling mixture, most of the high-boiling-point liquids will condense and flow back down the test-tube walls before they reach the upper part of the test tube. The thermometer in this apparatus is not used to measure the boiling temperature of the liquid, but serves to indicate when collecting tubes should be changed to receive different fractions.

Part C

Now fractionally distill about 25 cm³ of the liquid. Label the test tubes containing the fractions, so that you can keep track of them throughout the remainder of the experiment. Test each of the fractions for odor and flammability.

Part D

- Does sugar dissolve in fraction 1?
- What is the density of fraction 1?

Distill the fraction into a single test tube, recording the temperature of the vapor every half-minute until the fraction has nearly boiled away. Draw a vapor-temperature graph for fraction 1.

Part E

Repeat Part D for each of the other fractions.

Part F

Summarize your findings, and compare the odor, flammability, density, ability to dissolve sugar, and boiling point of each of the fractions and of the original mixture.

- What do you conclude about the composition of the fractions?
- Can you identify the substances in the mixture? (See Table 3.2, page 62.)
- What other tests might you make to help identify these substances?
- What do you think would happen if you were to re-distill each of the fractions separately?

1. In what characteristic property must two liquids differ if a mixture of them is to be separated by fractional distillation?

2. In the fractional distillation of liquids, which fraction has the highest boiling point? Which has the lowest boiling point?

3. The temperature-time graph shown in Figure A was made during the fractional distillation of a mixture of two liquids, *E* and *F*, and fractions were collected during the time intervals I, II, III, and IV. Liquid *E* has a higher boiling point than liquid *F*. What liquid or liquids were collected during each of the time intervals?

Figure A
For problem 3

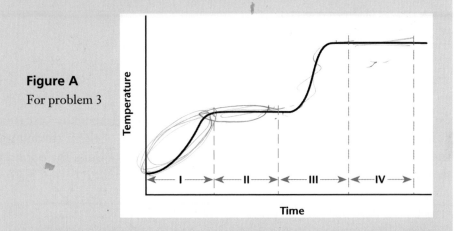

4. Suppose that when conducting Experiment 5.1, Fractional Distillation, a student collected two fractions, changing test tubes at the end of the first plateau. How would this have affected the composition of the two fractions?

5.2 Petroleum

It is not always easy to separate a mixture of liquids into pure substances by fractional distillation. If the boiling points of the substances in a mixture are nearly the same, they will all boil off together. In a liquid mixture containing many substances, some are sure to have boiling points close together. When we distill such a mixture, each fraction is made up of a number of different substances whose boiling points are close together. The first part to condense in one fraction may contain some of the substances that condensed in the last part of the previous fraction. However, the fractions that are more widely separated in boiling range are less likely to contain the same substances. Petroleum is an example of such a mixture. The compositions of typical fractions distilled from petroleum are shown in Table 5.1.

Table 5.1 A Few of the Substances Found in Petroleum

Substance	Density at 0°C (g/cm³)	Freezing point (°C)	Boiling point (°C)	Common products of petroleum		
				fuel gas	gasoline	kerosene
Methane	7.16×10^{-4}	−182.5	−161	X		
Ethane	1.35×10^{-3}	−183	−88	X		
Propane	2.02×10^{-3}	−190	−43	X		
Butane	2.68×10^{-3}	−138	−0.5	X		
Pentane	0.626	−129	36			
Hexane	0.660	−94	69		X	
Heptane	0.684	−90	98		X	
Octane	0.703	−57	125		X	
Nonane	0.722	−51	151		X	X
Decane	0.730	−30	174		X	X
Undecane	0.741	−26	196			X
Dodecane	0.750	−10	216			X
Tridecane	0.755	−5.5	236			X
Tetradecane	0.765	5.5	254			X
Pentadecane	0.776	10	271			X
Hexadecane	0.773	18	287			X

There are many more substances in the above products and in the higher-boiling-point fractions not listed in the table. Among these substances are fuel oils, lubricating oils, waxes, asphalt, and coke (mostly carbon).

Petroleum is believed to be produced naturally from vegetable and animal matter at the bottoms of shallow seas and swamps. When tiny plants and animals die in the sea, they settle slowly to the bottom, where they become trapped in mud and sand. This sediment of mud, sand, and dead organisms slowly becomes thicker and thicker. In a million years, it may become hundreds of meters deep. Such layers of sediment are very

Figure 5.2

A cross section of the earth's crust, showing how oil and natural gas are trapped in a porous rock layer by nonporous rock layers above and below. Note that well A produces only water, and well C produces only gas.

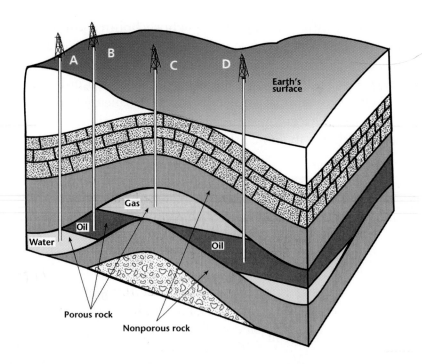

heavy, and the lower layers are compressed so much that they turn into rock layers. During this time, some of the body tissue of the entrapped organisms changes into a viscous, sticky liquid that is a mixture of many thousands of different substances. This liquid is called *petroleum* or *crude oil*. It is slowly squeezed out of the sediment in which it forms and eventually spreads through porous rock layers like water in a sponge.

In the course of more millions of years, the ever-changing crust of the earth—buckling in some places, rising in others, and sinking in still others—slowly moves and compresses the rock layers that were on the ocean bottom. Sometimes the porous oil-bearing rock is covered by a layer of hard, nonporous rock that has been bent into a dome or arch, as shown in Figure 5.2. Then the oil will be trapped, and cannot by itself squeeze to the surface. If it were not trapped, much of it would wash away and be lost.

Most of the petroleum in the earth's crust is stored by nature under formations of nonporous rock that trap the liquids below them. As Figure 5.2 shows, natural gas (the low-boiling-point substances in petroleum) and salt water from the sea are often trapped along with the oil. The nonporous "cap rock" may be hundreds of meters thick. It is expensive and difficult to drill through all this rock to get to the petroleum below, and it is not easy to predict where oil is trapped. Deep and expensive wells often fail to reach oil or gas. Some wells produce nothing but salt water, whereas others remain dry.

Petroleum was first discovered where it seeped to the surface in shallow pools. Once exposed to the air, some of the lower-boiling-point substances slowly evaporated, leaving behind tarry, almost solid asphalt. These tars, as well as the liquid petroleum, were used in the ancient world as mortar and embalming material.

One of the ancient methods used to distill crude oil consisted of heating the oil in a copper urn with a wool "sponge" at the narrow mouth of the vessel. The vapors condensed in the sponge, which was squeezed out into containers from time to time. A variation of this method made use of a heavy wick of wool that led from the mouth of the urn into a collecting vessel. Such a wick was a crude form of condenser.

The widespread use of kerosene lamps over 100 years ago—and the more recent use of gasoline engines—created a new demand for petroleum. This led to improved methods of locating oil and drilling wells. Also, better equipment was developed for fractionally distilling petroleum on a large scale (Figure 5.3).

A simplified diagram of this equipment, called a *fractionating column*, is shown in Figure 5.4. Heated crude oil enters the column near the bottom. The column contains a series of horizontal trays. As vapors from the heated liquid pass up through the column, the high-boiling-point

Figure 5.3

A fractional distillation column at a refinery.

Figure 5.4

A simplified diagram of a fractionating column used in the fractional distillation of petroleum.

substances condense in the lower, hotter trays. As the vapors move upward, they bubble through the liquid in the trays. In each tray, the condensing vapors increase the concentration of the substances whose boiling points are higher than the temperature of the tray. The rising vapors therefore become richer in the low-boiling-point substances. Some of the liquid that condenses in each tray overflows into the tray below, where it becomes heated again and re-distills. Each tray thus boils a particular mixture at a particular temperature. The temperatures of the trays and the boiling points of the substances in them decrease as one goes higher up the column.

Different fractions leave the column at different heights (Figure 5.4). Fractions with which you may be familiar are gasoline, kerosene, diesel fuel, heating and lubricating oils, paraffin, and asphalt.

5. Examine Table 5.1. What relationship can you identify between the densities of these substances and their freezing points? between densities and boiling points? between freezing points and boiling points?

6. a. In Table 5.1, which fractions would be liquid at room temperature (20°C)? Which would be solids? Which would be gases?

   b. You can see from the table that pentane is not an ingredient in any of the common products listed. What do you think accounts for this?

7. A sample of crude oil is boiled for several minutes. What change takes place in its density? (See Table 5.1.)

5.3 The Separation of Insoluble Solids

Solids with a density greater than that of water sink in water, and those with a lesser density float, provided they are insoluble. We can use this fact to separate a mixture of sawdust and sand. After stirring the mixture in water, we can skim off the floating sawdust. Then we can pour off the water and dry the sand.

This method is called *separation by flotation* and is widely used in industry to concentrate ores. For example, a common copper ore, copper sulfide, is usually found mixed with large amounts of worthless rock. The ore is finely ground, and then mixed with water and selected substances that produce a heavy foam when the mixture is agitated violently with air. The copper sulfide is contained in the floating foam; the ground rock settles. The foam is removed, and the copper sulfide is recovered.

8. Sawdust and sand can be separated by flotation in water. Could sawdust from two different woods that had densities of 0.6 and 0.9 g/cm³ be separated by flotation in water? by flotation in decane (see Table 5.1)?

9. The example in Section 5.3 of separating sand and sawdust requires that the substances have different densities. What needs to be true about their solubilities for this process to work?

no, both of them can float; yes in decane

the one that needs to float has to be insoluble

EXPERIMENT

5.4 The Separation of a Mixture of Solids

Examine the mixture of solids supplied by your teacher. If one solid is soluble in water and the other is not, you can separate them easily by dissolving one and separating it from the other by filtering. You can do this in the following way: Put about 1.5 g of the mixture into a test tube, and add 5 cm³ of water. Stopper the test tube, and shake it for several minutes.

- Do you think either substance dissolved?

To find out, filter out the undissolved solid, as shown in Figure 5.5. Wash the precipitate on the filter paper by pouring an additional 10 cm³ of water into the funnel. You can now put about 5 cm³ of the clear liquid—the filtrate—into an evaporating dish and boil it to dryness.

- Have the two substances been separated?

Filter paper

Funnel

Filtrate

Figure 5.5

Filtering a liquid. The filter paper is folded into a cone, which fits snugly into the funnel.

° mix w/water
(dissolves a solid)
° boil off to
dryness

10. In what characteristic property must two solids differ if they are to be separated merely by being dissolved at room temperature and filtered?

11. Much salt is obtained from salt mines, in which great masses of salt occur mixed with insoluble earthy impurities. What steps can be taken to purify the salt?

12. How can drinking water be obtained from seawater?

5.5 The Separation of a Mixture of Soluble Solids

In the previous experiment, you were able to separate two solids because one of them was soluble in water and the other was not. How can a mixture of two soluble solids be separated? To illustrate the method of separation, consider a mixture of 8.0 g of sodium chloride and 5.0 g of potassium nitrate. At room temperature these two substances have nearly the same solubility (Figure 5.6). Therefore, at room temperature both the 8.0 g of sodium chloride and the 5.0 g of potassium nitrate will dissolve.

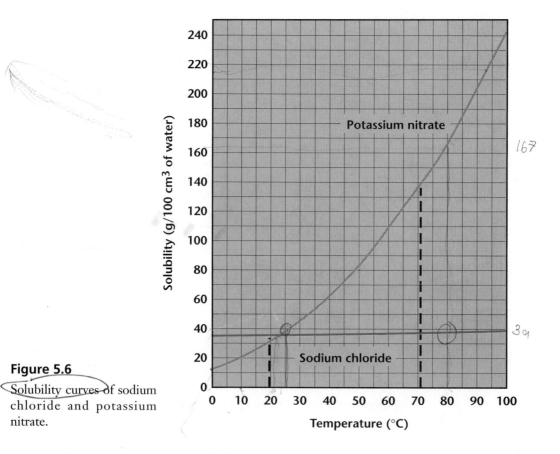

Figure 5.6

Solubility curves of sodium chloride and potassium nitrate.

Suppose we dissolve the mixture in water at 70°C. At this temperature, the solubility of potassium nitrate is much greater than that of sodium chloride. If we use just enough water to dissolve the potassium nitrate at 70°C, most of the sodium chloride will remain undissolved and can be filtered out.

After filtering, we let the solution cool down to room temperature. Almost all the sodium chloride will remain in solution, because its solubility hardly changes with temperature. However, the solubility of potassium nitrate is much lower at room temperature than at 70°C. Therefore, as the solution cools, potassium nitrate will precipitate out of the solution and can be filtered out. This process, called *fractional crystallization*, is summarized in Figure 5.7. By repeated fractional crystallizations, even solids whose solubilities are very close to each other at room temperature can be separated.

(a) At 70°C

In solution:
All of potassium nitrate
Some of sodium chloride

Solid:
Most of sodium chloride

(b) Filtered at 70°C

Solid (on filter paper):
Most of sodium chloride

In solution:
All of potassium nitrate
Some of sodium chloride

(c) Standing at room temperature

Solid:
Most of potassium nitrate

In solution:
Some of potassium nitrate
Some of sodium chloride

(d) Filtered at room temperature

Solid (on filter paper):
Most of potassium nitrate

In solution:
Some potassium nitrate
Some sodium chloride

Figure 5.7

A diagram of the series of steps for separating a mixture of sodium chloride and potassium nitrate.

To achieve a better understanding of the process, we shall review it using the solubility values from Figure 5.6. At 70°C the solubility of potassium nitrate is 138 g/100 cm³. That is, 100 cm³ of water will dissolve 138 g of potassium nitrate. To dissolve 5.0 g of potassium nitrate will require

$$100 \text{ cm}^3 \cdot \frac{5.0 \text{ g}}{138 \text{ g}} = 3.6 \text{ cm}^3.$$

The 5.0 g of potassium nitrate is mixed with 8.0 g of sodium chloride. How much sodium chloride will dissolve in 3.6 cm³ of water? Figure 5.6 tells us that to dissolve 38 g of sodium chloride at 70°C requires 100 cm³ of water. Therefore, in 3.6 cm³ of water only

$$38 \text{ g} \cdot \frac{3.6 \text{ cm}^3}{100 \text{ cm}^3} = 1.4 \text{ g}$$

of sodium chloride will dissolve with the potassium nitrate. The remaining 6.6 g of sodium chloride in the original mixture can be filtered out.

When the filtered solution is cooled down to room temperature, almost all of the 1.4 g of sodium chloride will remain dissolved. How much of the 5.0 g of potassium nitrate will precipitate? At 22°C the solubility of potassium nitrate is 37 g/100 cm³. (Again, see Figure 5.6.) The 3.6 cm³ of water in which the 5.0 g of potassium nitrate was originally dissolved at 70°C will now dissolve only

$$37 \text{ g} \cdot \frac{3.6 \text{ cm}^3}{100 \text{ cm}^3} = 1.3 \text{ g}$$

of potassium nitrate, and 3.7 g will be filtered out. Thus, 6.6 g of sodium chloride and 3.7 g of potassium nitrate have been separated from the mixture. Only 1.4 g of sodium chloride and 1.3 g of potassium nitrate remain in the solution. By repeated fractional crystallizations, the two substances can be separated further.

13. Suppose two substances have the same solubility in water at all temperatures. Can they be separated by fractional crystallization? Why or why not?

14. Suppose you wish to separate more of the two solids, sodium chloride and potassium nitrate, remaining in solution, as described at the end of Section 5.5. How should you proceed to do this?

15. Suppose that you planned to separate a mixture of 8 g of sodium chloride and 5 g of potassium nitrate at 80°C rather than at 70°C. How would this higher temperature affect the separation of the two solids in this mixture?

16. What temperature should you choose to precipitate potassium nitrate from a saturated solution of sodium chloride when the two are present in equal amounts in a mixture? Explain.

17. Would being able to control the temperature of the funnel used to separate a mixture of soluble solids by fractional crystallization help to effect a better separation? Why or why not?

EXPERIMENT

5.6 Paper Chromatography

So far you have learned how differences in density, boiling point, and solubility can be used to separate substances. In this experiment you will investigate a method that works even when the substances in the mixture are present in only minute quantities.

In a plastic bottle containing water, hang a strip of filter paper streaked with green ink from a felt-tip pen, as shown in Figure 5.8. When the color has risen up the paper to about 2 or 3 cm below the top, remove the paper and hang it up to dry.

Figure 5.8

One method of making a paper chromatograph. The point of the filter-paper strip extends into the water so that the ink streak is about 1 cm above the water. The strip is held in place by a stopper.

- How many different substances can you identify?
- Can you put the substances back together again to make green ink?

Cut out each of the colored sections, and put each one in a separate test tube. Add between 0.5 cm³ and 1 cm³ of water to each tube.

- Do the colored substances dissolve?

Pour the liquids from all three test tubes into a single test tube.

- What color is produced?

5.7 A Mixture of Gases: Nitrogen and Oxygen

So far in this chapter you have learned how to separate mixtures of liquids, mixtures of solids and liquids, and mixtures of solids. We have not yet considered the separation of mixtures of gases. If a gas is dissolved in a liquid, all we have to do is heat the mixture. The solubility of gases decreases with temperature (Table 4.2, page 82).

For example, when a glass of cold water warms up to room temperature, bubbles of air appear on the sides of the glass. If the water is warmed further, more air bubbles appear, and some rise to the top long before the water reaches its boiling point. Separating mixtures of gases alone, however, requires different methods from those used so far.

Mixtures of gases are very common. Table 5.1 lists four gases that are mixed together in the petroleum fraction called "fuel gas."

There are a number of ways to separate gases. One of them, which is widely used, is to cool the mixture until it condenses to form a liquid. Then we can make use of the different boiling points of the various liquids and fractionally distill the cold liquid. The gases are thus collected one by one, as the boiling temperature levels off at new plateaus.

Air that is liquified and fractionally distilled in this way separates mainly into two fractions: A glowing splint bursts into a bright flame when placed in one of them, but even a splint that is burning brightly goes out when placed in the other. The gas that causes the glowing splint to burst into flame is oxygen, and the one that does not is nitrogen. These two gases together make up about 99 percent of the gases in air. Nitrogen makes up about 80 percent of the atmosphere, and oxygen about 20 percent. The densities, melting points, and boiling points of nitrogen and oxygen are given in Table 5.2.

The cheapest way of obtaining oxygen and nitrogen is to condense air into a liquid and then fractionally distill it. Most of the oxygen and nitrogen commercially manufactured is produced by this method.

Table 5.2

Gas	Density (g/cm³)	Melting point (°C)	Boiling point (°C)
Nitrogen	1.2×10^{-3}	−210	−196
Oxygen	1.3×10^{-3}	−218	−183
Hydrogen	8.4×10^{-5}	−259	−253

The densities are given for atmospheric pressure and room temperature.

18. **To what temperature should a mixture of nitrogen and oxygen be cooled in order to separate them using fractional distillation?**

19. **Could nitrogen, oxygen, and hydrogen occur together in a mixture of liquids?**

20. **How can you separate propane gas from air?**

5.8 Mixtures and Pure Substances

In this chapter we have found ways to separate different substances from each other by using characteristic properties. A difference in density can be used to separate two solids; solids can also be separated by differences in solubility. A difference in the boiling points of different liquids enables us to separate them by fractional distillation.

Suppose we experiment with a piece of solid material to see if we can separate it into two or more substances. First we grind it up and mix it with water, stirring it thoroughly. We observe that some particles of a yellowish solid float on the surface, while particles of a gray solid sink to the bottom. We skim off the floating material, whose density is obviously less than that of water. We dry it, label it fraction 1, and set it aside. Then we filter the water and the more dense solid that is in the bottom of the test tube. This solid, which remains on the filter paper, we dry, label fraction 2, and set aside also. We know that these two solids, fractions 1 and 2, are different substances, because they have different densities.

We now test the filtrate to see if any material has dissolved in the water. When we evaporate the water, we find a small amount of white solid. This substance, which is different from both fractions 1 and 2 because it is soluble in water, we call fraction 3. The whole process of

Solid material

Ground up

Mixed with water

Floaters skimmed

Floaters dried

Fraction 1

Some solid sinks

Filtered residue

Fraction 2

Water filtered

Dissolved material evaporated to dryness

Water evaporated

Fraction 3

Figure 5.9

A diagram of an example of the series of steps for separating three fractions obtained from a ground-up solid.

the separation of three fractions from a piece of solid material is diagrammed in Figure 5.9.

We now have separated three different substances, but perhaps each of these can be further separated. To find out, we use other separation methods. We may, for example, try to melt and even fractionally distill each of the fractions, or we may try dissolving them in different liquids. Suppose that boiling, melting, and mixing with alcohol and other liquids do not produce anything with characteristic properties different from those of the three original fractions. By using all these various tools of separation again and again, we find that the characteristic properties of our three fractions remain unaltered. We call such substances whose properties are not changed by repeating any of these procedures *pure substances*.

Suppose we mix together all the pure substances that we obtain in this way. If the resulting material has the same characteristic properties as the original sample, we can say that the original sample was a *mixture* of the pure substances. For example, if you mixed all the fractions you separated in Experiment 5.1, Fractional Distillation, you would end up with a substance that has the same properties with which you started. Similarly, mixing together the various fractions obtained from the distillation of liquid air would yield a gas with exactly the same properties as ordinary air. Therefore, air is a mixture.

Note that many properties of a mixture are intermediate between the properties of the pure substances that form the mixture. For example, the density of air is between the density of nitrogen and that of oxygen. A mixture of alcohol and water will smell like alcohol, but it will burn only if it contains enough alcohol.

---

21. Suppose a mixture is separated and found to contain iron filings, salt, and sulfur. If the same amounts of these three substances are mixed together again, will the new mixture have the same properties as the original mixture? *yes*

22. Consider two mixtures of nitrogen and oxygen; one is 5% nitrogen and the other is 50% nitrogen. Do the two mixtures have identical characteristic properties? *no, b/c the amt of nitrogen is different*

23. Suppose you mixed together all the fractions from the fractional distillation of the liquid in Experiment 5.1, Fractional Distillation. What do you think would be the properties of this liquid?

24. A sample of a liquid was boiled for 12 minutes. During that time, the boiling point remained constant, and the volume was reduced to half. Is the liquid a pure substance?

25. In earlier times people would search out sandy stream beds in which small particles of gold were mixed with the sand. They separated this gold from the sand by "panning." Find out how this was done. What characteristic property of the substances made panning possible?

26. Figure 5.2 shows gas, oil, and water trapped below a nonporous rock layer. Why is the layer of water below the oil and the layer of gas above the oil?

27. Figure 5.2 shows four oil wells drilled into oil-bearing porous rock. Can you suggest some method, other than drilling deeper, for getting more oil from well D after the oil level drops below the end of the well?

28. Using the data in Table 5.1 (page 93), draw and label a possible distillation curve for a mixture of hexane, nonane, and tetra-decane.

29. Oil and vinegar are often served as salad dressing. They can be poured into the pitcher shown in Figure B. The pitcher has a spout on each side. Yet, oil comes out on one side and vinegar on the other. How do you think the pitcher works?

Figure B
For problem 29

30. a. If a solution containing 40 g of potassium nitrate in 100 cm³ of water at 100°C is cooled to 25°C, how much potassium nitrate will precipitate out of solution? (See Figure 5.6.)

    b. Suppose that the 40 g of potassium nitrate is dissolved in only 50 cm³ of water at 100°C. How much potassium nitrate will precipitate out if the solution is cooled to 25°C?

31. Suppose you dissolve 30 g of sodium chloride in 100 cm³ of water at 100°C and boil away 50 cm³ of the water.

a. How many grams of sodium chloride will remain in solution?

b. How many grams will precipitate out of solution?

32. Suppose you dissolve 40 g of potassium nitrate in 100 cm³ of water at 100°C.

a. If half the solution is poured out, how many grams of potassium nitrate will the remaining solution contain?

b. Now, instead of pouring out part of the solution, you boil away 50 cm³ of water. How many grams of potassium nitrate will remain in solution at 100°C?

c. If the solution remaining in (b) were cooled to 25°C, how much potassium nitrate would precipitate out of solution?

33. When ethanol is to be used for industrial or commercial purposes other than as a beverage, it is customarily denatured. What, in general, do you think some of the properties of the added substance might be?

34. How could you separate a mixture of powdered sugar and powdered citric acid?

35. The mineral called "Gay-Lussite" appears to be a pure substance, but it is actually a mixture composed of calcium carbonate (limestone), sodium carbonate (soda ash), and water. Describe how you could go about separating these three substances from the rock. Some of the properties of calcium carbonate and sodium carbonate are listed in the following table.

Property	Calcium carbonate	Sodium carbonate
Melting point	Decomposes at 825°C	851°C
Solubility in alcohol	Insoluble	Insoluble
Solubility in hydrochloric acid	Soluble	Soluble
Solubility in water	Insoluble	7 g/100 cm³ at 0°C; 45 g/100 cm³ at 100°C

36. You can use paper chromatography to separate the components in many common substances. Try this technique with any of these substances found at home: tomato paste, different colors and brands of ink, the coloring in leaves and vegetables (grind the leaves first and dissolve them in alcohol), and flower petals.

37. Chlorophyll can be extracted from leaves by grinding them with alcohol to give a dark-green solution. By careful application of paper chromatography, bands of yellow and red color, as well as green bands, can be detected. What other reason do you have to suspect the presence of substances producing these colors in leaves? Why do you ordinarily not see them?

38. As liquid air boils away, the remaining liquid becomes richer in one of the two gases—nitrogen or oxygen. Which one is it? How do you know?

39. What should you do to separate
    a. alcohol from water?
    b. sodium chloride from sodium nitrate?
    c. nitrogen from oxygen?

Theme for a Short Essay

You devoted several hours to the "sludge test." Do you think this test is a good way to assess your progress in this course? Why, or why not? Include enough information about the test so that a friend who has never heard about the "sludge test" will be able to understand your reasoning.

6 Compounds and Elements

6.1 Breaking Down Pure Substances

It is not always possible to restore an original sample by mixing the parts separated by the various processes described in Chapter 5. A simple example of a substance that breaks up when heated and that is not a mixture is mercuric oxide, an orange powder. If you try to determine its melting point, you will discover that when it is heated, mercuric oxide gives off a gas. If you test this gas, you will find it to be oxygen. Furthermore, you can detect some droplets of a silvery liquid—mercury—in the test tube. Mixing the oxygen and the mercury together, however, will not restore the mercuric oxide. The two components remain separated as a gas and a silvery liquid.

Mercuric oxide is a pure substance that cannot be separated into simpler substances by most of the methods we used to separate mixtures. Once mercuric oxide has been separated by heating, it cannot be put back together simply by mixing.

Similarly, baking soda, which you heated at the beginning of the course, is also a pure substance. It decomposed into a solid, a liquid, and a gas. If you had tested these remaining substances, you would have found them also to be pure substances. Mixing them will not bring back the baking soda.

Heating is not the only method for decomposing a pure substance. In the next section, you will use a different method.

E X P E R I M E N T
6.2 The Decomposition of Water

Water is one of the pure substances you have separated out of many mixtures. But water itself cannot be separated into other substances by the methods used in the previous chapter. After heating, distilling, and freezing water, we always end up with plain water. To separate water into simpler substances, we shall need a new method, different from any used so far. Such a method, developed at the beginning of the nineteenth century, relies on electricity and is called *electrolysis*.

⚠ CAUTION: Be sure to wear safety glasses.

Set up the apparatus shown in Figure 6.1. Connect the wires to the battery and see if anything happens. Since this reaction is very slow when pure water is used, something must be added to speed up the process. Try adding from 10 to 30 cm^3 of sodium carbonate solution to the water.

Figure 6.1

Apparatus for decomposing water. The electrodes are clamped alongside the inverted test tubes and connected to a battery (not shown). Any gas that forms on either of the stainless-steel electrode tips will be collected when it rises and displaces water from its test tube. No reaction is observed until a small amount of sodium carbonate solution is added to the water.

Disconnect the battery when one of the test tubes is nearly full of gas. Mark the volume of gas in each tube with a grease pencil or rubber band.

You have probably heard that water is made up of hydrogen and oxygen. Recall that a glowing splint bursts into a bright flame when placed in oxygen (Section 5.7). On the other hand, hydrogen will burn (or pop) in the presence of a flaming splint. Test the gases to see if you come to the same conclusion using flaming and glowing splints. Be sure to remove the test tubes from the water in such a way that you do not lose any gas.

Measure the volumes of the gases in the test tubes. To compare these two volumes, divide the volume of the hydrogen by the volume of the oxygen. This gives you the ratio of the volume of hydrogen to the volume of oxygen. Compare your ratio with the ratios obtained by students who used different amounts of sodium carbonate solution mixed with the water.

- Does the amount of solution added to the water affect the volume ratio?
- Using Table 3.1, what is the mass ratio of hydrogen to oxygen?

A pure substance that can be broken up into two or more pure substances is called a *compound*. The characteristic properties of a compound are quite different from those of its components.

1. Suppose that during Experiment 6.2, some oxygen gas was inadvertently bubbled outside of the test tube. How would this affect the calculated volume ratio of hydrogen to oxygen?

   oxygen would decrease, ratio would increase

2. Suppose that when conducting Experiment 6.2, a student allows the hydrogen gas to completely fill the test tube to the point of overflow. How does this error affect the volume ratio of hydrogen to oxygen that the student determines?

   hydrogen would decrease, ratio decrease

3. Does the volume of hydrogen plus the volume of oxygen collected in Experiment 6.2 equal the volume of water broken down?

4. a. What is the combined mass of oxygen and hydrogen that can be produced by the decomposition of 180 g of water by electrolysis?
   b. If all the hydrogen produced in part (a) were burned in air to form water, what mass of water would result?

5. In decomposing water, suppose you had filled many test tubes with gas. As the water disappeared from the beaker, suppose you refilled it without adding more sodium carbonate. You would have found that the ratio of hydrogen to oxygen produced remained constant. What does this tell you about the source of the gases? about the sodium carbonate?

   gases did not come from sodium carbonate

6. What would be the ratio of the volumes of gas in the two test tubes if you had interchanged the connections to the terminals of the battery halfway through the experiment? *the sodium carbonates speeds up the process of electrolysis*

6.3 The Synthesis of Water

In the last experiment, you could have mixed oxygen and hydrogen gas together in a test tube. Nothing would have happened unless you had ignited the mixture. Then a violent reaction would have occurred. With the proper equipment, the gases could have been separated before ignition by cooling them down until the oxygen condensed at −183°C, leav-

chemical 3
physical

[compound]
H2O
*/ *
2   1 Oxygen
hydrogen

pure
substances

ex.
4 h + 1 ox = 1
-2   H2O
___
2h + O ox

the ratio never changes

ing the hydrogen as a gas. But this method would not have worked if the mixture of gases had first been ignited. As a result of the ignition, the two gases would have combined to form a compound, water vapor, that cannot be separated into hydrogen and oxygen by condensation. The combining of substances to form a compound is called *synthesis*. This process is the opposite of decomposition.

When you electrolyzed water, you found the ratio of the volume of hydrogen to the volume of oxygen produced. No matter how much water you decomposed, the ratio remained the same. Of course, you might have expected this, since all the water you used came from the same source. But can hydrogen and oxygen combine in different proportions, or will they combine only in the same volume ratio?

To answer this question, we could try adding different volumes of hydrogen to a fixed volume of oxygen, igniting each mixture, and measuring how much of each gas, if any, remains uncombined. We have done this experiment. First we filled a special shock-resistant glass tube with water and inverted it in a tray of water. A volume V of oxygen was then bubbled into the bottom of the tube. The oxygen rose to the top, as shown in the tube on the left in Figure 6.2(a) on the next page. (The water levels are marked by rubber bands.)

We then added a volume V of hydrogen to the same tube (the tube in the center). Next, we ignited the mixture of gases by sending an electric spark through the mixture. After ignition, we measured the volume of gas that remained unreacted (the tube on the right).

In Figure 6.2(a), the volume of hydrogen added was equal to the volume of oxygen. After ignition, a volume of gas equal to $1/2V$ did not react.

In Figure 6.2(b), the volume of hydrogen used was $2V$, or twice the volume of oxygen. In this case, practically all of the mixture reacted.

In Figure 6.2(c), the volume of hydrogen added before ignition was $3V$. A volume equal to $1V$ of gas did not react.

From Figure 6.2, you can see that the ratios of the volumes of hydrogen to oxygen before ignition in (a), (b), and (c) were 1/1, 2/1, and 3/1, respectively. When tested after ignition, the gas remaining in (a) was oxygen and that in (c) was hydrogen. (The volume of the bubble remaining in (b) was too small to identify the gas.) The increased amount of water in the tubes came from the tray of water. The water produced in the reactions amounted to only a few drops.

The results of this experiment are summarized in Table 6.1 on page 115. As you can see, the ratio of the volume of hydrogen to the volume of oxygen that combined to form water was the same in each case, regardless of the ratio of the volumes of the two gases in the mixture before they were ignited by an electric spark.

Figure 6.2

In each of the three parts of this figure, (a), (b), and (c), the tube on the left was first full of water (not shown). Then, a volume V of oxygen was bubbled into the bottom of the tube. The open (lower) end of the tube is submerged in water.

(a) An equal volume of hydrogen was added to the oxygen, and the mixture was ignited by an electric spark. Note that about $\frac{1}{2}V$ of gas remained unreacted.

1 : 1

(b) A volume $2V$ of hydrogen was added. All the gas reacted. (The tiny bubble is within the uncertainty of the volume measurements.)

2 : 1

(c) A volume $3V$ of hydrogen was added to the oxygen. Now a volume equal to $1V$ remained unreacted.

1V of oxygen + **1V of hydrogen** → **Result: ½V of gas left**

1V of oxygen + **2V of hydrogen** → **Result: no gas left**

1V of oxygen + **3V of hydrogen** → **Result: 1V of gas left**

Table 6.1

Tube	Initial volume of oxygen (cm³)	Initial volume of hydrogen (cm³)	Final volume of gas (cm³)	Volume of oxygen that combined (cm³)	Volume of hydrogen that combined (cm³)	Ratio of hydrogen to oxygen
1	25.0 / 2	25.0	12.4 oxygen	12.6	25.0	1.98
2	25.0	50.0	0.8	25.0	49.2*	1.97
3	25.0	75.0	24.6 hydrogen	25.0	50.4	2.02

*For the purpose of calculation, we assume the remaining bubble to be hydrogen. In all likelihood, it is a mixture of hydrogen and oxygen.

This ratio is the same as the ratio of hydrogen gas to oxygen gas obtained by the careful electrolysis of water in Experiment 6.2, The Decomposition of Water. The experiment in Figure 6.2 shows what happens to any excess gas. Over the range of volumes used, if the volume of either gas was greater than the volume needed for a hydrogen-to-oxygen ratio of 2:1, only part of the gas reacted. The excess gas remained uncombined.

7. Suppose three tubes are filled with a mixture of hydrogen and oxygen in a manner similar to that used in Figure 6.2. The tubes contain the volumes of hydrogen and oxygen shown in the table below:

Tube	Volume of oxygen (cm³)	Volume of hydrogen (cm³)
I	25	75
II	50	50
III	25	50

After the mixture in each tube has been ignited, which of the following represents the volume and the identity of the unreacted gases in tube I? in tube II? in tube III?
A. 25 cm³ of oxygen
B. 50 cm³ of hydrogen
C. 25 cm³ of hydrogen
D. No unreacted gas

tube I = C
tube II = a
tube III = d

8. If 18 g of water is decomposed into hydrogen and oxygen by electrolysis, 16 g of oxygen and 2 g of hydrogen are produced. Using the densities in Table 3.1 (page 52), find (a) the volume of water decomposed and (b) the volume of hydrogen produced.

18 cm³

2 3.×10⁴

18 g × $\frac{1 cm^3}{1 g}$ = 18 cm³

2 g × 1 cm³

.000004

2.3 × 10⁴

9. Suppose you were not told the identity of the gases that remained unreacted in the experiment shown in Figure 6.2. Suggest a line of reasoning that would lead to the conclusion that the remaining gas in part (*a*) is oxygen, and in part (*c*) is hydrogen.

10. Suppose you mixed 100 cm³ of oxygen with 200 cm³ of hydrogen. The volumes of both gases are measured at atmospheric pressure and 20° C.
    a. Calculate the mass of oxygen and the mass of hydrogen used.
    b. If you ignited the mixture, what mass of water would result from the reaction?
    c. What volume of water would be produced?

11. If in problem 10 you had used 100 cm³ of oxygen but only 50 cm³ of hydrogen, what mass of water would have resulted?

EXPERIMENT

6.4 The Synthesis of Zinc Chloride

You have learned that hydrogen and oxygen combine in a definite ratio, no matter how much of each mix together and ignite. That reaction involves two gases. You will now investigate what happens when a metal reacts with an acid: in this case, zinc with hydrochloric acid. Will a given amount of zinc always react with the same amount of hydrochloric acid?

Everyone in your class will use the same amount of hydrochloric acid, but different groups will add different amounts of zinc. When the reaction is complete, you will determine the mass of zinc that reacted. You will then evaporate the remaining liquid and mass the solid residue. Then each group will calculate the ratio of the mass of zinc reacted to the mass of solid product formed (the solid is called *zinc chloride*).

The reaction between the zinc and the acid will produce much heat. To keep the mixture cool, you can perform the reaction in a large test tube placed in a beaker of cold water (Figure 6.3).

Mass an exact amount of zinc between 0.5 g and 4 g. Place the zinc in a test tube and add 10.0 cm³ of hydrochloric acid.

⚠ **CAUTION: Always wear safety glasses when you work with acids. Be careful not to spill any of the solution on your books or clothes. If some acid spills on your hands, wash them thoroughly with water.**

• What is the gas given off in the reaction?

Figure 6.3

Zinc is placed in 10.0 cm³ of hydrochloric acid in a test tube, which is placed in a beaker of cold water to keep the solution from becoming too hot.

The reaction at first is quite vigorous. However, to make sure that it is complete, allow the mixture of zinc and acid to stand overnight. In the next period, pour the liquid from the test tube into an evaporating dish that you have already massed. If there is still zinc left over from the reaction, be sure the solid stays in the test tube when you pour the solution. Wash the test tube, and any zinc remaining, with 5 cm³ of water.

- Why should you add the washing water to the evaporating dish?

Dry the leftover zinc, and mass it.

- How much metal reacted with the hydrochloric acid?

The evaporating dish can be placed on a burner stand and heated, as shown in Figure 6.4. If the solution begins to spatter, gently move the flame back and forth.

Heat the material until it appears to be dry. Continue heating until the solid begins to melt and a tiny pool of liquid forms in the bottom of the evaporating dish. You can mass the dish and its contents as soon as they have cooled.

- What is the ratio of the mass of zinc reacted to the mass of zinc chloride formed?
- Compare your results with those of your classmates. Did an excess of either zinc or hydrochloric acid affect your results?
- If the zinc chloride were not completely dry when massed, how would this affect your ratio?

Figure 6.4

Evaporating a solution in an evaporating dish heated directly over an alcohol burner or a microburner.

12. How would the mass ratio of the zinc reacted to the zinc chloride be affected if the zinc chloride were not thoroughly washed from the test tube into the evaporating dish?

13. What would be the ratio of zinc to zinc chloride if 5.00 g of zinc reacted during Experiment 6.4?

14. Which of the following calculations can you use to determine the mass of the zinc chloride produced when 5.00 g of zinc reacted?
    A. 5.00 g × 0.48
    B. 5.00 g ÷ 0.48
    C. 0.48 ÷ 5.00 g

15. In a certain package of seed corn, there were 36 red seeds and 24 yellow seeds. In a second package, the number of red seeds was 51 and the number of yellow seeds was 34.
    a. What is the ratio of the number of red seeds to the number of yellow seeds in each package?
    b. What is the ratio of the number of red seeds to the total number of seeds in each package?

16. Suppose that there are 10 boys and 15 girls in a class.
    a. What is the ratio of boys to girls in the class?
    b. What is the ratio of boys to the total number of students in the class?
    c. What would be the ratio of boys to girls if the class were three times larger but the ratio of boys to the total number of students were the same?

17. When various amounts of zinc react with hydrochloric acid, zinc chloride and hydrogen are produced. Which of the following ratios between the masses of various products and reacting substances are constant regardless of the amounts of zinc and acid mixed together?

A. $\dfrac{\text{Zinc added}}{\text{Zinc chloride produced}}$ B. $\dfrac{\text{Zinc used up}}{\text{Hydrochloric acid used up}}$

C. $\dfrac{\text{Zinc used up}}{\text{Hydrogen produced}}$ D. $\dfrac{\text{Zinc used up}}{\text{Zinc chloride produced}}$

E. $\dfrac{\text{Zinc added}}{\text{Hydrochloric acid added}}$ F. $\dfrac{\text{Zinc chloride produced}}{\text{Zinc used up}}$

6.5 The Law of Constant Proportions

In the last two sections, you studied the synthesis of two compounds: water from oxygen and hydrogen, and zinc chloride from zinc and hydrochloric acid. You found that hydrogen and oxygen combine only in the definite mass ratio of 0.13. It does not matter in what proportion these gases are mixed. When they are ignited, the hydrogen and oxygen that react do so in a definite proportion to produce water. In the last experiment, zinc chloride was produced when zinc combined with the chlorine in the hydrochloric acid. The ratio of the mass of zinc that reacted to the mass of zinc chloride was constant. It was independent of an excess either of hydrochloric acid or of zinc. This means that the ratio of zinc to the chlorine with which it combined also was constant.

We consider both water and zinc chloride to be compounds and not mixtures because the characteristic properties of each are quite different from those of the substances from which it is made. Do all substances combine in a constant proportion when they form compounds?

When you investigated the law of conservation of mass, there were two experiments in which compounds were formed. In one of these (Experiment 2.5), you heated copper and sulfur to make a new substance. Suppose we repeat the experiment, keeping the mass of copper constant and varying the mass of sulfur. Will we find that the mass of copper that reacts remains in a constant ratio to the mass of the product, independent of how much sulfur we use?

This experiment has been done many times. As long as there is more than enough copper to react with all the sulfur, the ratio of the mass of the copper that undergoes reaction to the mass of the product remains fixed. However, as additional amounts of sulfur are used, a point is eventually reached when the ratio is no longer fixed but decreases. A greater mass of sulfur seems to react with the same mass of copper, yielding a lower value for the ratio of the mass of the copper reacted to the mass of the product. In this case it appears at first that when copper and sulfur combine to form a compound, the ratio of the masses that react can vary.

The early chemists strongly disagreed about the relative amounts of substances that react to form compounds. On one side was a distinguished French chemist, Claude Louis Berthollet (1748–1822). He claimed, on the basis of experiments like the one with copper and sulfur, that a pair of substances can combine in any proportion to form a compound. On the other side was another distinguished French chemist, Joseph Louis Proust (1754–1826). He based his answer on evidence obtained from experiments that showed constant proportion, like the synthesis of water and of zinc chloride.

Proust suggested a new law of nature, *the law of constant proportions*, which he stated thus in 1799: "We must recognize an invisible hand which holds the balance in the formation of compounds. A compound is a substance to which Nature assigns fixed ratios; it is, in short, a being which Nature never creates other than balance in hand." In plainer language, the law that Proust formulated can be stated as follows: When two substances combine to form a compound, they combine in a constant proportion. The ratio of the masses that react remains constant, no matter in what proportions the substances are mixed. If there is too much of one of the substances in the mixture, some of it just will not react.

When the law of constant proportions was formulated, the evidence in its favor was much weaker than the evidence you gathered for the law of conservation of mass at the end of Chapter 2. In spite of much evidence that supported Berthollet's stand and that Proust could not explain, Proust was confident enough to claim constant proportions as a law of nature.

The explanation of results like those in the copper/sulfur reaction that seemed to support Berthollet's stand will be discussed later in the course.

EXPERIMENT

6.6 A Reaction with Copper

Some substances react very fast. As you learned in Section 6.3, when a test tube of hydrogen and oxygen is ignited, the reaction is extremely rapid. Indeed, it is explosive and ends in a fraction of a second. Solids usually do not react as fast as gases. In this experiment you will investigate how the reaction of finely ground copper with oxygen in the air proceeds with time.

Mass a dry crucible and add about 1 g of copper dust. Now find, as accurately as possible, the total mass of the copper and the crucible.

Heat the copper, as shown in Figure 6.5, for 2 minutes. While heating, watch the copper carefully.

⚠ CAUTION: Always wear safety glasses when you use a burner.

- Does a reaction take place?

When the crucible is cool, mass the crucible and its contents.

- Did the crucible and its contents gain or lose mass?
- Is your answer to the previous question evidence that a reaction has taken place?

Figure 6.5

Powdered copper in a crucible supported by a triangle over a microburner. The wires of the triangle are bent so that they can be hooked into holes in the pegboard for rigid support.

• What do you predict will happen if you continue to heat the crucible for an additional 10 to 15 minutes? Try it.

Break up the contents of the crucible with a scoopula and examine the pieces.

• Do you think that all the copper has reacted? If not, what fraction do you estimate did not react?

NOTE: Do not discard the black solid in your crucible. Pour the pieces of solid into a test tube and save them for use in the next experiment.

EXPERIMENT

6.7 The Separation of a Mixture of Copper Oxide and Copper

Suppose all the copper that you started with in the preceding experiment had reacted with oxygen. In that case the black solid present at the end of the experiment would be the pure substance copper oxide. If, however, not all the copper reacted, then the black solid would be a mixture of copper and copper oxide. In order to determine whether the black solid is a mixture, you will attempt to separate it.

A good way to separate a mixture like copper oxide and copper is to place the mixture in a solvent that will dissolve one of the components but not the other. Copper will not easily dissolve in hydrochloric acid, as your teacher can show you. Copper oxide, on the other hand, is soluble in hydrochloric acid.

Place in a test tube all the black solid you obtained in the previous experiment. Add 5 cm³ of hydrochloric acid and stir gently with a glass stirring rod for 5 to 10 minutes. See the "CAUTION" on the next page.

> ⚠ **CAUTION: Always wear safety glasses when you work with acids. Be careful not to get any hydrochloric acid on yourself or your books or clothes. If some acid spills on your hands, wash them thoroughly with water.**

After letting the solid settle to the bottom, slowly pour off the liquid into another test tube. Now wash the remaining solid several times with water and discard the wash water.

- What does the remaining solid look like?
- Is the black substance a mixture?

> **NOTE: Do not discard the acid solution. You will need it for the next experiment.**

> 18. Compare the method of separating the black solid mixture in this experiment and the method of separating a mixture of solids in Experiment 5.4. How are they similar? How are they different?

6.8 Complete and Incomplete Reactions

Many reactions, like the reaction of copper with oxygen, are slow. It is difficult in such cases to tell when one of the reacting substances has been completely used up. Because the copper in your crucible changed to a black solid, you may have assumed that *all* the copper had reacted. This would have been an incorrect assumption, as the presence of copper in the black substance has shown.

Reactions like the reaction of copper with oxygen are called *incomplete reactions*, because neither one of the reacting substances, copper or oxygen, is completely used up during the reaction. Other reactions, for example, the reaction of zinc with hydrochloric acid, which you studied in Section 6.4, are *complete reactions*. Zinc will continue to react with hydrochloric acid until either one of the two has been completely used up.

Recall the controversy that existed among early chemists about the validity of the law of constant proportions (Section 6.5). At least part of the controversy could have been avoided if they had more carefully analyzed their experiments. Some of their disagreements occurred because they did not understand the difference between complete and incomplete reactions. Specifically, they often mistook the masses they mixed for the masses that reacted. As your own experience shows, this mistake is easy to make.

EXPERIMENT

6.9 Precipitating Copper

When you heated a sample of finely ground copper in Experiment 6.6, A Reaction with Copper, you observed an increase in mass. This indicated that something was being added to the copper. A new substance, copper oxide, was formed. In Experiment 6.7, The Separation of a Mixture of Copper Oxide and Copper, you dissolved the copper oxide in hydrochloric acid, and from the black powder you produced a blue-green solution.

What happened to the copper in all these reactions? Did it disappear forever, or is it still in the solution in some form? Putting a piece of zinc in the solution will provide you with an answer. As you already know, zinc in hydrochloric acid will generate heat.

! CAUTION: Always wear safety glasses when you work with acids. Put the test tube containing the solution in a beaker half-filled with water.

Put a piece of zinc in the solution you saved from Experiment 6.7, and observe the reaction. While the reaction is going on, break up the solid from time to time with a stirring rod.

After the zinc has finished reacting, pour off the solution from the remaining solid and wash the solid several times with water to clean off the acid. Remove the washed solid from the test tube and dry it quickly by pressing it between two layers of paper towel.

Press a scoopula firmly against the paper towel and move it across the dry solid.

• Can you identify the solid?

20. What would happen if you heated the solid that you recovered in this experiment?

21. How do you expect the total mass of solid recovered in Experiments 6.7 and 6.9 to compare with the initial mass of copper you heated in Experiment 6.6?

6.10 Elements

Heating copper in air is not the only way to produce a reaction with copper. There are many other reactions, and they all have one feature in common: The product of the reaction always has a larger mass than the mass of copper. Neither heating nor electrolysis will change copper into something that has a smaller mass than did the copper with which we started.

Now we will contrast this behavior of copper with that of mercuric oxide (Section 6.1). When you heat mercuric oxide, oxygen is given off, and the resulting mercury has a smaller mass than the original quantity of mercuric oxide. We reason, therefore, that mercury is a simpler substance than mercuric oxide.

In Experiment 6.2, The Decomposition of Water, you electrolyzed water, causing it to decompose into hydrogen and oxygen. In the same way, molten sodium chloride can be decomposed by electrolysis into chlorine and sodium. The mass of either the chlorine alone or the sodium alone is less than the mass of the sodium chloride from which they were produced. Thus, sodium and chlorine must be simpler substances than sodium chloride. However, just as with copper, none of the methods that can be used to break up other substances work for either sodium or chlorine. Pure substances that do not break up by heating, electrolysis, reacting with acids, or similar methods are called *elements*.

It is not necessary, of course, to try to break up the many thousands of pure substances in order to find out which of them are elements. In many cases we know substances are compounds simply because they can be made by combining other substances. For example, we can "burn" sodium in an atmosphere of chlorine gas. The resulting white solid has the characteristic properties of table salt. Thus, table salt is not an element. It is the compound sodium chloride.

Early chemists using this reasoning were able to identify as possible elements a relatively small number of the pure substances they knew. One such list, proposed by the French chemist Antoine Lavoisier in 1789, was accompanied by the following explanation: "Since we have not hitherto discovered the means of separating them, they act with regard to us as simple substances, and we ought never to suppose them compounded until experiment and observation have proved them to be so."

Lavoisier's list of elements included several well-known substances that are also found on today's list of elements. Among them are iron, copper, silver, gold, hydrogen, oxygen, and carbon. From a historical point of view, two substances are of special interest. One was on Lavoisier's list and one was not.

The first substance is lime, which can be produced by strongly heating limestone. Lime was known to the Romans as early as 200 B.C.E. Many attempts were made over the years to decompose lime: The substance was heated in air, heated in a vacuum, and heated with carbon. Every attempt failed, and most people agreed that lime must be an element. There were a few doubters, who thought that lime was probably a compound of a metal with oxygen. They reasoned that lime could not be decomposed simply because the usual agent, carbon, which worked with copper oxide and other oxides, was somehow not "powerful" enough to separate the oxygen from the metal.

As so often happens, a new discovery had to wait for a new experimental method. In this case, the electric battery, invented by Alessandro Volta in 1800, was the necessary tool. In 1807, the English chemist Humphry Davy used an electric battery to try to decompose metal oxides. He had already used a battery to decompose molten potash and molten soda to obtain the new elements potassium and sodium. A similar procedure failed to work with lime because lime could not be melted. After much experimentation, however, Davy finally succeeded. He was able, by carefully electrolyzing moist lime, to produce tiny amounts of a new element he called *calcium*.

Missing from Lavoisier's list was a very reactive gas, slightly green in color. It was discovered in 1774 as a by-product of some experiments with muriatic acid. (Muriatic acid we now call hydrochloric acid.) Various people experimented with the new gas and found it similar in many ways to the gases from other strong acids. Acids were considered in those days to be substances that were strongly corrosive and had a sour taste. Since oxygen was believed at that time to be the active ingredient in all acids, this new substance was named "oxymuriatic acid gas."

This name stuck for more than thirty years, mainly because it had been suggested by some very important and respected chemists. Several people tried, unsuccessfully, to decompose the gas. They always blamed their failures on poor methods and poor tools. In 1810 Humphry Davy, after working with his usual patience and brilliance for a full two years, finally announced the results of his long series of experiments. These experiments, Davy wrote, ". . . incline me to believe that the body improperly called oxymuriatic acid gas has not as yet been decompounded; but that it is a peculiar substance, elementary as far as our knowledge extends, and similar in many of its properties to oxygen gas. . . ." In order that people would no longer be misled into thinking it a compound, he suggested a new name, "based upon one of its obvious and characteristic properties—its color," and called it *chlorine*. Davy's conclusion has stood the tests both of time and of new techniques, and chlorine is included in the present-day list of elements.

22. Which of the following can you use to demonstrate that the iron found in a sample of iron oxide is an element and not a compound?

A. The mass of the iron oxide is greater than the mass of the iron alone.

B. Iron is shiny while iron oxide is not.

C. Iron cannot be broken down into simpler substances.

23. How do you know that water, zinc chloride, and baking soda are not elements?

24. Hydrogen chloride—a gaseous pure substance—can be decomposed into two different gases, each of which acts like a pure substance. On the basis of this evidence alone:

a. Can hydrogen chloride be an element?

b. Can either of the other two gases be an element?

c. Can you be sure that any of the pure substances mentioned is an element?

25. While on a class field trip, a student found a shiny rock that appeared to be a metal. When she returned to the classroom, she heated the rock for a while and found that it lost mass. Further heating did not affect the mass. Could this rock be an element? Explain your answer.

26. Explain in your own words how you would decide that a pure substance is an element and not a compound.

6.11 Elements near the Surface of the Earth

Of the 112 elements known today, only about 50 elements are commonly used; they are listed in Table 6.2. The elements on the left side of the table are listed in decreasing order of abundance near the surface of the earth. The elements on the right side of the table are listed alphabetically; their abundance is less than that of argon and is not listed.

The part of the earth for which abundance was calculated includes the atmosphere, the oceans, and the ground to a depth of one kilometer below the surface (including that below the oceans). The data used in the calculations are based on the analysis of thousands of samples of soil, sea water, and air collected at many locations.

Note how few elements account for most of the mass around us. The first five elements (oxygen to iron) in the left-hand column of Table 6.2 account for almost 92 percent of the total mass of the elements found near the surface of the earth. Oxygen, the most abundant element, occurs in many compounds found in the ground. Ordinary sand contains mostly silicon dioxide, a compound of oxygen and silicon. Silicon dioxide is also the main ingredient of glass. Hydrogen, the third element in Table 6.2, is found primarily in the oceans. The 62 elements not listed in the table together account for less than 0.001 percent of the mass near the earth's surface.

Table 6.2 Elements Found near the Surface of the Earth

Name	Symbol	Abundance (in % by mass)	Name	Symbol
Oxygen	O	65.5	Arsenic	As
Silicon	Si	13.7	Boron	B
Hydrogen	H	5.4	Bromine	Br
Aluminum	Al	4.2	Cadmium	Cd
Iron	Fe	3.1	Cesium	Cs
Calcium	Ca	2.4	Cobalt	Co
Sodium	Na	1.7	Germanium	Ge
Magnesium	Mg	1.5	Gold	Au
Chlorine	Cl	0.95	Helium	He
Potassium	K	0.94	Iodine	I
Titanium	Ti	0.32	Krypton	Kr
Nitrogen	N	0.14	Lead	Pb
Sulfur	S	0.061	Lithium	Li
Phosphorus	P	0.060	Mercury	Hg
Manganese	Mn	0.053	Neon	Ne
Fluorine	F	0.028	Osmium	Os
Barium	Ba	0.020	Platinum	Pt
Strontium	Sr	0.019	Polonium	Po
Carbon	C	0.010	Radium	Ra
Vanadium	V	0.0067	Radon	Rn
Chromium	Cr	0.0060	Silver	Ag
Nickel	Ni	0.0050	Tin	Sn
Zinc	Zn	0.0039	Tungsten	W
Copper	Cu	0.0034	Uranium	U
Argon	Ar	0.0023	Xenon	Xe

27. Oxygen comprises only about 20 percent of the air by mass. How can you account for the fact that oxygen makes up 65.5 percent of the mass for which abundance was calculated in Table 6.2?

28. How many elements collectively compose 99 percent of the mass of the earth accessible to people?

29. Data for the elemental composition of living matter were not used to calculate the abundance of the elements that are listed in Table 6.2. Even so, the data in Table 6.2 are correct. How do you think that this can be so?

30. The total mass of the one-kilometer layer of ground, the oceans, and the atmosphere is 2.8×10^{21} kg. What is the mass of (a) iron, (b) sulfur, and (c) copper near the surface of the earth?

31. For which of the elements listed in Table 6.2 have you held or seen samples?

▶ For Review, Applications, and Extensions

32. Suppose that the apparatus you used in Experiment 6.2, The Decomposition of Water, contained 100 cm³ of water. Using this apparatus, a student collected 57 cm³ of hydrogen and 28 cm³ of oxygen. What fraction of the total volume of water was decomposed?

33. A paint manufacturer takes great care to make the ingredients and their relative amounts always the same for each particular color of paint. Although the composition of a particular paint does not change, why is the paint not a compound?

34. A mass of 5.00 g of oxygen combines with 37.2 g of uranium to form uranium oxide.
    a. How many grams of the oxide are formed?
    b. What is the ratio of uranium to oxygen in this compound?
    c. How much oxygen is needed to oxidize completely 100 g of uranium?

35. Is the melting point of zinc chloride lower than the temperature of your burner flame?

36. When you make a solution of salt and water, over what range of values can you vary the mass ratio of salt to water at a given temperature?

37. Compare the method of separating the black solid mixture in Experiment 6.7 with the method used to separate a mixture of solids in Experiment 5.4. How are they different?

38. Discuss the process of boiling an egg in terms of complete and incomplete reactions. What may affect the time required for a complete reaction?

39. What evidence do you have for each of the following statements?
    a. Zinc chloride is a pure substance and not a mixture.
    b. Water is a pure substance.

40. A student heated a crucible containing 2.15 g of powdered copper until the mass of the contents of the crucible became 2.42 g. The black solid in the crucible was then placed in hydrochloric acid, and 1.08 g of copper remained undissolved in the acid. What is the reacting ratio by mass of copper with oxygen?

41. Hydrochloric acid is a water solution of the compound hydrogen chloride. Suppose there were two bottles containing hydrochloric acid in your lab. How could you determine whether the concentration of hydrogen chloride in each bottle is the same?

42. a. If you heat a piece of blue vitriol (a blue solid), mass decreases and the solid changes to a white powder. Which of the two substances might be an element?
    b. If you dissolve the white powder in water and place an iron nail (iron is an element) in the solution, the nail will become coated with a thin layer of copper. What can you now conclude about the two substances in part (a)? Is either of them an element?

43. Silicon is one of the most abundant elements near the surface of the earth. However, few people have seen or could recognize a sample of silicon. Why do you think this is so?

THEMES FOR SHORT ESSAYS

1. "Seeing is believing" is a common saying. But does "not seeing" imply "not believing"? Neither hydrogen nor oxygen is visible in Figure 6.2 or in the laboratory. Is there, perhaps, a form of indirect seeing? Express your thoughts on this subject.

2. Express the main points of Section 6.5 as a debate between Berthollet and Proust.

7 Radioactivity

7.1 Radioactive Elements

You have now reached a high point in your study of matter. Through simple experiments, you have traced the main steps leading to a recognition of how the material world is put together. The accomplishments of the past few centuries are really impressive: The millions of mixtures around us are now known to be made up of tens of thousands of compounds, which in turn are composed of only about a hundred elements. Compounds have characteristic properties that are different from those of the elements from which they are made. Yet the elements never really disappear. They can always be extracted from their compounds. Elements seem to be permanent.

In science, however, it often happens that a new observation is made just when we think that our understanding of a subject is complete. This observation forces us to admit that our picture is incomplete; some new features must be added.

In the case of elements, some substances that qualified as elements were found to be *not* permanent, but to change on their own into other elements. The ground-breaking experiment leading to this discovery was made by the French physicist Henri Becquerel over a hundred years ago. We shall now describe a modern version of his experiment.

Six plastic boxes containing samples of different materials were placed on photographic film. The film was wrapped in black paper to shield it from light. After three days the film was developed. Figure 7.1 shows where the boxes were placed. Figure 7.2 shows three white squares on the developed film where boxes *A*, *C*, and *E* were placed. Apparently, the material in these boxes gave off something that was able to get through the black paper and affect the film in the way that light does.

Figure 7.1

Six different substances in small plastic boxes are placed on photographic film enclosed in black paper. The boxes are left in position for three days before the film is developed and the photograph produced.

Figure 7.2

The finished photograph from Figure 7.1. The three white squares appear where boxes *A*, **C**, and *E* were placed.

The elements contained in the boxes (all are in compounds, except in box *F*) are listed in Table 7.1. Boxes *A* and *B* had two elements in common: sulfur and oxygen. However, box *A*, not box *B*, affected the film. This suggests that uranium was the element that emitted, or *radiated*, something. This conclusion is supported by the fact that box *C*, which also contained uranium, left a mark on the photographic film.

Similarly, a comparison of the contents of boxes *D* and *E* suggests that the thorium in box *E* is the cause of the mark on the film.

Photographic film is not the only tool that distinguishes boxes *A*, *C*, and *E* from the others. If we place any one of these boxes near an

table 7.1	
Box	**Elements**
A	Uranium, sulfur, oxygen
B	Sodium, sulfur, oxygen
C	Uranium, nitrogen, oxygen
D	Sodium, nitrogen, oxygen
E	Thorium, nitrogen, oxygen
F	Sulfur

Figure 7.3

A Geiger counter used to detect radiation from radioactive substances. The detector, next to the yellow sample, is connected to a computer, which serves as a recorder.

instrument called a Geiger counter (Figure 7.3), the counter will count or produce clicks that can be counted. Boxes *B*, *D*, and *F* do not affect the counter at all.

There are other elements found near the surface of the earth (listed in Table 6.2) that radiate something that affects a photographic plate and a Geiger counter. These elements are called *radioactive* elements.

1. Elements *X*, *Y*, and *Z* form compounds *XY*, *XZ*, and *YZ*. Compounds *XY* and *YZ* are radioactive but *XZ* is not. Which element is radioactive?

2. Does the radiation emitted by uranium compounds depend upon elements other than uranium that are present in the compounds?

3. An experiment similar to the one described in Figures 7.1 and 7.2 showed that a compound of polonium, sulfur, and oxygen is radioactive. Which of the three elements must be radioactive?

4. A piece of zinc placed in hydrochloric acid causes hydrogen to be released. Evaporation of the resulting solution leaves behind a white solid. A similar reaction occurs when a piece of uranium is placed in hydrochloric acid. Do you expect this white solid to be radioactive?

7.2 Radioactive Decomposition

What happens to a radioactive element when it radiates? This is a hard question to answer. Some elements, such as uranium, radiate so weakly that it is extremely difficult to discover what is happening to them. Other radioactive elements, such as polonium, emit such intense radiation that it is a simple task to determine what happens. However, because of its intense radiation, even a milligram (10^{-3} g) of polonium is a health hazard unless special precautions are taken.

Despite the difficulties, both weakly and strongly radiating elements have been studied using a variety of methods. One method, spectral analysis, will be discussed in Chapter 8. In the case of polonium, spectral analysis shows that the radiation is associated with changing polonium into lead and helium. Spectral analysis shows that other radioactive elements also change into different elements. In many cases, helium is one of the elements that is produced. Whether helium is produced or not, we refer to this process as *radioactive decomposition* or *radioactive decay*.

Is radioactive decomposition different from the decomposition of water or other compounds? You saw that the products of the decomposition of water could be recombined to form the original compound. Lime, which Lavoisier thought to be an element, is very difficult to decompose into calcium and oxygen even by electrolysis. Nevertheless, calcium and oxygen easily recombine to form lime. It has been possible to recombine all the elements that have been obtained from compounds. However, no one has been able to recombine the products of radioactive decomposition by using the methods that are effective in recombining elements into compounds.

What happens to a radioactive element when it is heated? Does heat change the rate at which it emits radiation? In many of the experiments you have done and read about in this course, temperature has had a big effect on what happened and how fast it happened. Baking soda emitted a gas only when you heated it. Hydrogen does not burn by itself in air, but when it is heated with a burning match, it catches fire very easily— sometimes explosively.

The effect of temperature on the rate at which radiation is emitted by radioactive substances has been studied. Samples of the substances were heated to very high temperatures and cooled to very low temperatures. Temperature had no effect on the radiation from a radioactive substance.

To sum up, radioactive elements have all the properties of elements that you studied in the preceding chapters. They form compounds with constant proportions, and they have characteristic densities, melting points, and boiling points. They cannot be decomposed by ordinary heat, electricity, reaction with acids, and the like. They differ from nonradioactive elements in that they affect a photographic plate and decompose into other elements. The rate at which they decompose cannot be changed by any of the means that affect the rate at which compounds decompose. That is why these substances are called elements; but to set them apart, we call them radioactive elements.

5. Suppose the boxes shown in Figure 7.1 were cooled below the freezing point of water. How would this have affected the appearance of the photographic film shown in Figure 7.2?

6. What are the two most important differences between the following two reactions?
   a. Water → hydrogen + oxygen
   b. Polonium → lead + helium

7. A radioactive sample at 20°C is placed near a Geiger counter. The counter records 1.0×10^2 counts per minute. The temperature of the sample is then raised to 100°C. What does the counter then record?

EXPERIMENT

7.3 Radioactive Background

When a Geiger counter is placed near a radioactive substance it registers decays. What do you expect a counter to read if no known radioactive substance is nearby?

When there is only one Geiger counter per class, each of you may be assigned different tasks in this class experiment. Set up a Geiger counter in your classroom and let it count for 1.0 minute. Reset the counter and take two or three additional readings for one minute each.

• What was the number of counts in each reading? Were the readings all the same?

Let the counter run for 30 minutes.

• What was the average number of counts per minute over the 30-minute interval?

The average number of counts per minute registered by a counter when no obvious radioactive source is present is called the *radioactive background*, or *background* for short.

The background may depend on location and, in a closed space, on ventilation. Repeat the background measurement in the basement or other room chosen by your teacher.

• What was the background in the basement or other room?

8. In an experiment to determine the radioactive background, a Geiger counter detected 940 counts during 60.0 minutes. Which of the following should you report for the radioactive background?
   A. 15.7 counts/min
   B. 31.3 counts/min
   C. 28,200 counts/min

9. A student measured the radioactive background in two locations. At location A she observed 50 counts in 2.0 minutes, and at location B, 150 counts in 10.0 minutes. Which location had the higher background?

10. Six readings of a Geiger counter were taken over 1-minute intervals. The numbers of counts per minute were: 12, 14, 15, 9, 7, and 18. What do you think the result of the next reading would have been? Why?

EXPERIMENT

7.4 Collecting Radioactive Material on a Filter

You may or may not be able to tell whether the background in the basement is significantly higher than in your classroom. But you can find out if the background radiation in the basement has the same origin as the background radiation upstairs. The radiation can come down from the sky, it can come up from inside the earth, or it can come from radioactive material floating in the air.

Suppose the source is dust in the air. It may be possible to catch some of this dust by passing a large volume of air through a filter. You can do this by fastening a piece of paper towel around the end of the tube of a vacuum cleaner (Figure 7.4). After the air has flowed through the filter for a time set by your teacher, turn off the vacuum cleaner and place the Geiger counter in

Figure 7.4

The end of a tube of a vacuum cleaner covered with a piece of paper towel serving as a filter.

Figure 7.5

The loaded filter and the Geiger counter.

front of the filter for 3 or 4 minutes (Figure 7.5). Dividing the number of counts by the time during which they were collected gives the *counting rate*.

- How does the counting rate compare with the background when classroom air passed through the filter?
- How does the counting rate compare with the background in the basement when basement air passed through the filter?
- What do you conclude about the source of the extra counts?

The counting rate that you have measured so far includes the background. To find the counting rate due to the radioactive material, subtract the background from the measured counting rate. The difference is called the *net counting rate*. Whenever the measured counting rate is large compared with the background, the net counting rate will be close to the measured one. However, when the measured counting rate is close to the background, the net counting rate will be close to zero.

11. The counting rate near a radioactive source was 49 counts/min. When the source was removed, the counting rate dropped to 21 counts/min. Which of the following was the net counting rate of the source in counts/min?

    A. 21   B. 28

    C. 49   D. 70

12. A laboratory group found the background in a basement to be 15 counts/min and the counting rate for basement air passed through a filter to be 176 counts/min. What should the group report for the net counting rate in the basement?

13. A class had the following results when collecting radioactive material on a filter: in a closed basement closet, 412 counts in 2.00 minutes; on an open terrace, 36 counts in 2.00 minutes. A background of 19 counts/min was found from an earlier run that lasted 30.0 minutes.

    a. What were the two measured counting rates in counts per minute?

    b. What were the two net counting rates?

    c. If one of the net counting rates were negative, how would you explain such a result?

14. Suppose the net counting rate determined when basement air passed through a filter was close to zero. What would you expect to find for the net counting rate if you repeated the experiment outside or in the classroom? Give your reasoning.

EXPERIMENT

7.5 Absorption and Decay

Keeping the filter and the counter in fixed positions, hold one, two, or more pieces of paper between them, and measure the counting rate. For reasons that will become clear very shortly, these measurements are best done in rapid succession.

- Does the paper affect the net counting rate? If so, how?

- Which has the greater effect on the net counting rate, a few pieces of paper or a sheet of aluminum?

Measure the counting rate two more times, at about 20 minutes and 40 minutes after the first measurement. (The exact times are not important as long as you keep a record of what they were.) Taking the time of the first measurement as zero, plot the net counting rate as a function of time. Your data may look somewhat like those in Figure 7.6 (on the next page): the counting rate decreases with time, but apparently in an irregular way. Can we represent such data by a smooth curve?

There is a difference between plotting radioactivity measurements and, say, mass measurements. Massing a test tube several times will give the same results within the sensitivity of the balance. For example, the results may vary between 23.24 g and 23.26 g. However, a mass of 15.85 g would clearly indicate an error in reading or a malfunction of the balance. The

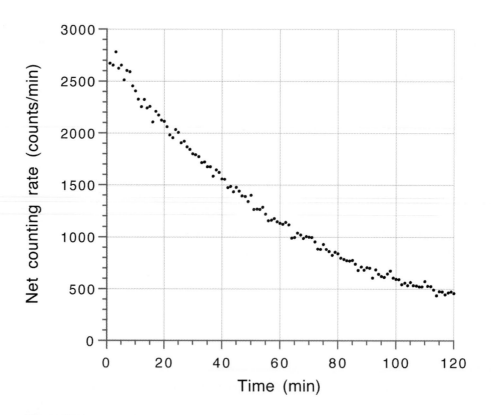

Figure 7.6

Actual class data for the net counting rate for radioactive material collected on a paper filter.

results of counting-rate measurements are quite different. Background measurements over short time intervals vary considerably. The same is true for the net decay rate of a radioactive substance. Another run under the same conditions would produce different numbers showing only the same general trend.

Therefore, it makes no sense to try to draw a curve through all the data points. A smooth curve that has about the same number of data points on each side is likely to fit different sets of data and so be more representative. Figure 7.7 shows such a curve. Other curves close to the one in Figure 7.7 would also be acceptable.

Draw a smooth curve for your net counting rate as a function of time.

- How long did it take for the net counting rate to decrease to half its original value? from half the original value to a quarter?
- Do you see any relation between these two time intervals?
- What net counting rate do you expect to find after one day?

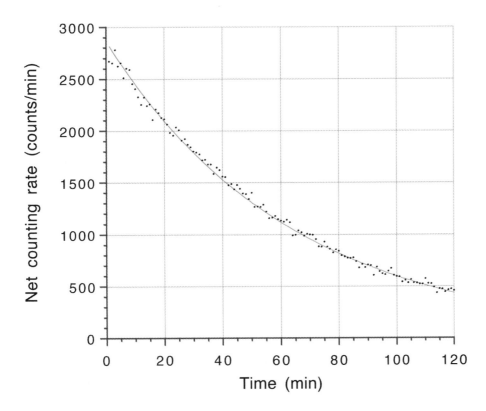

Figure 7.7

A smooth line has been drawn close to the data points in Figure 7.6. The fact that the first and last points are closest to the curve is accidental.

15. In Figure 7.7, how long did it take for the net counting rate to decrease to half its original value? from half the original value to a quarter?

16. Figure A is a graph of the net counting rate as a function of time for a sample of polonium.

   a. How long did it take for the counting rate to decrease to half its original value? from half the original value to a quarter?

   b. How are these two time intervals related?

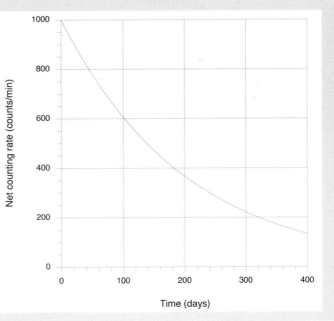

Figure A

For problem 16

17. Suppose a filter used to collect radioactive dust is made of two layers of paper towel. The two pieces of paper are placed in front of identical Geiger counters for the same length of time. Which layer, the outer or the inner, will produce the greater number of counts? Explain your reasoning.

7.6 A Closer Look at Radioactivity

So far we have observed some general features of radioactive decay. Now we shall take a closer look at how it happens. We begin with the effect of a radioactive element on photographic film. Look again at Figure 7.2 on page 133. The two white squares and the gray square appear uniform.

A similar experiment was done using a very small sample of polonium. Three photographic plates were exposed to radiation in the arrangement shown in Figure 7.8. The plates were exposed for 66, 94, and 144 hours, respectively. When the developed plates were examined, the first one showed a very light uniform gray spot, the second had a darker shade, and the third was still darker.

When the center of each of the spots was photographed through a high-powered microscope with a magnification of about 10^3, none of them appeared to be a uniform shade (Figure 7.9). In all the photographs, the dots are about equal in size and blackness, and form no particular pattern. They appear to be distributed in a random way. On the more exposed plates, there are, on average, more black dots in each square.

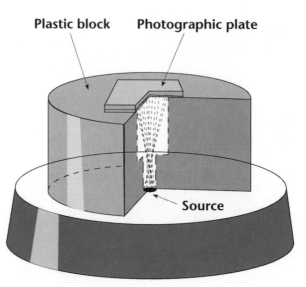

Plastic block **Photographic plate**

Source

Figure 7.8

A photographic plate exposed to a tiny amount of polonium.

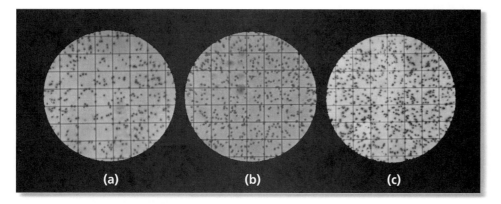

Figure 7.9

Three photographic negatives obtained with the apparatus shown in Figure 7.8. The three pictures show very small, equal-sized areas of the negatives, magnified a thousand times. Negatives (a), (b), and (c) were exposed for 66, 94, and 144 hours, respectively.

When a Geiger counter is close to a radioactive sample, you hear distinct clicks. The clicks occur at random. Even after listening for hours, you would not be able to predict when the next click would come. We can be confident about only the average number of clicks in any given time interval.

A more vivid picture of radioactive decay is provided by a device called a *cloud chamber* (Figure 7.10). Figure 7.11 on the next page shows a photograph of a cloud chamber that contains a sample of polonium. You can

Figure 7.10

A simple cloud chamber. The chamber itself is a cylindrical plastic box resting on a block of Dry Ice. A dark felt band soaked in isopropanol encircles the inside of the top of the chamber. The bottom of the chamber is painted black so that the white fog track will be clearly visible from above. The chamber is illuminated from the side. The radioactive source is on the tip of the needle.

Figure 7.11

see individual tracks originating from the sample. The tracks are formed instantaneously—as far as one can tell just by looking. Nevertheless, it seems reasonable that they are formed by very fast particles flying off from the radioactive source.

Watching a cloud chamber in operation, you will notice that the tracks shoot off irregularly. Just as with the black dots on the film and the clicks of the counter, you will not be able to predict when and in which direction the next track will appear. Only the average number of tracks produced in a long time interval can be predicted from past observations.

This kind of behavior is characteristic of events that happen by chance. For example, suppose you throw 10 dice many times. In each throw of 10 dice, you are likely to find one or two sixes. In some cases you will find three or more sixes, or none at all. You have no way of telling what the next throw will produce. However, the average number of sixes in many throws of ten dice can be predicted to be 10/6.

The manner in which film, Geiger counters, and especially cloud chambers record radioactive decomposition suggests that this process takes place in discrete, or countable, steps. Each black dot, click, or track signals the arrival of a small particle emitted by the radioactive source. Combining this idea with the fact that elements are produced during radioactive decomposition leads to a far-reaching conclusion: Elements are made up of discrete units, or some sort of tiny particles, called *atoms*.

Historically, the idea that elements are made up of atoms preceded the discovery of radioactivity. We have chosen to introduce this idea through radioactivity because radioactivity enables us to count individual events in which elements are changed.

18. Having observed a cloud chamber and a Geiger counter near a radioactive source, which of the following can you predict?

    A. The next track only

    B. The next click only

    C. Both of these events

    D. Neither of these events

19. Can you tell whether the tracks in Figure 7.11 are slanting upward, are slanting downward, or are horizontal? What assumption are you making in arriving at your answer?

20. Summarize the similarities between radioactive decay as observed with a cloud chamber and with a Geiger counter.

21. State in your own words why radioactive decomposition suggests that elements are made of tiny particles.

7.7 Radioactivity and Health

When the radiation from radioactive substances hits photographic film, it makes some changes in the film. If it did not, the film could not serve as a detector. When the same radiation hits other materials, it also causes some changes. If the material hit is a human body, the changes can be harmful if the radiation is sufficiently strong. How deep into the body does the radiation found in basements penetrate?

The thickness of a layer that is needed to absorb most of the radiation from a particular source depends on the source and the absorber. Some of the radiation found in basements cannot even enter a common Geiger counter, although the front of the counter has a very thin cover. This radiation can be detected only by special counters. Some radioactive materials must be placed behind a thick wall to provide effective shielding.

What is the danger from the radiation found in basements? The observation that even a piece of paper absorbs a noticeable fraction of the radiation suggests that much will be stopped by the clothing and the skin. However, our lungs have no skin to protect them. They have a large surface area for the exchange of oxygen and carbon dioxide. Between inhaling and exhaling, radioactive material in the air can be deposited on the surface of the lungs. If the concentration of radioactive material in the air is large enough and the air is breathed over a long enough time, the danger of lung cancer cannot be ignored.

Figure 7.12

A comparison between irradiated (right) and nonirradiated strawberries (left). Both samples were kept under refrigeration for two weeks beneath a plastic cover. (*Courtesy International Atomic Energy Agency*)

Why is the danger mostly in basements? A radioactive gas called *radon* originates inside the earth. Radon is an element, which, like helium and neon, does not form compounds. If it reaches the surface of the earth, it will enter the atmosphere. If it reaches a basement, its concentration will rise, because basements are entered less often and are not as well ventilated as upstairs rooms. The radiation emitted by radon is of the kind that is not detected by most Geiger counters. What you observed was the radiation emitted by the decay products of radon.

In general, the concentration of radioactive material in the air of a basement is small. This is why we needed a vacuum cleaner to collect enough radioactive material from a large volume of air.

Just as radiation from radioactive substances can be harmful to humans, it also destroys the bacteria that cause fruits to rot and milk to spoil. In recent years irradiation has increasingly been used to preserve food products. Products preserved in this way do not contain any chemical additives (Figure 7.12).

For Review, Applications, and Extensions

22. A plant absorbs various substances through its roots. Different elements of these substances concentrate in different parts of the plant. Suppose one of these elements is radioactive. How would you determine in what parts of the plant it concentrates?

23. a. With a paper towel in place, it took a small vacuum cleaner 32 seconds to fill a 160-liter plastic bag with air. How much air passed through the filter in 1 second? in 1 minute?

    b. Suppose you had used the vacuum cleaner from part (a) to perform Experiment 7.4. How much air would pass through the filter in the time you collected the radioactive material?

24. Which could you predict with more confidence?

    A. The time between two consecutive automobile collisions at a busy intersection.

    B. The total number of collisions per year at the same intersection.

25. a. Breathe normally into a small plastic bag and estimate the volume of air that you exhale in one breath.

    b. Count how many times you exhale per minute (breathing normally).

    c. What volume of air passes through your lungs each minute?

    d. Suppose you stayed in the basement for the same period of time that it took to collect the radioactive material in Experiment 7.4. How much air would pass through your lungs?

    e. Suppose that your lungs act like the combination of filter and counter used in Experiment 7.4. What would be the "counting rate" of your lungs due to breathing the basement air?

26. In the *IPS* video "Radioactive Substances I," the Geiger counter counted much faster when box *A* was placed next to it than when box *E* was. Is this what you would have expected on the basis of the brightness of the white squares in Figure 7.2? Why or why not?

27. The *IPS* video "Radioactive Substances II" shows tracks being produced in a cloud chamber. From what you see in the loop, can you be sure that the tracks start at the source rather than end there? What does this tell you about the speed of the particles that leave the tracks?

THEMES FOR SHORT ESSAYS

1. The use of fluoride to reduce tooth decay was quite contro-versial in the past. Today, irradiating fruits and vegetables to reduce spoilage is controversial. Interview your teachers, parents, and friends to assess their feelings on this issue. Try to determine the basis for these feelings.

2. "Background" radiation is a metaphorical term borrowed from the arts, including theater and painting. Write your thoughts on how background radiation is both similar to and different from the background in a theatrical production.

8 The Atomic Model of Matter

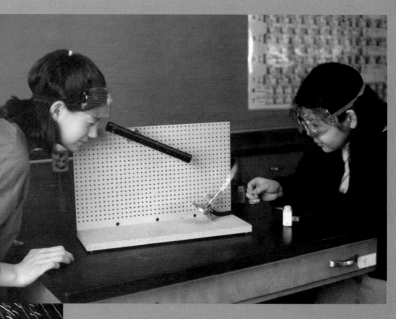

8.1 A Model

Suppose someone hands you a sealed can. You shake it, and hear and feel something sloshing around inside. From this simple experiment you can form a mental picture—a *model*—of what is inside the can. You conclude that the can contains a liquid. You have no knowledge about the color, taste, or odor of the liquid. But you are sure that the contents of the can has a characteristic property of liquids—it sloshes around when you shake the can. The "liquid model" of the can accounts for your observation.

However, for a model to be useful, it has to offer more than just a convenient way of accounting for known facts. A model must also enable us to make testable predictions. For example, from the "liquid model" of the can, we can make the following prediction: If you punch a small hole in the bottom of the can, liquid will drip out.

The simple model we have made for the behavior of the can was the result of just one experiment, shaking the can. It led to only one rather obvious prediction. Before we go on to develop an atomic model of matter, you will do an experiment with a "black box." This experiment will give you an opportunity to develop a richer model than the one offered by the can. It will also make it easier for you to understand the atomic model of matter.

1. **A good model enables us to summarize and account for the facts we learned from observation and experiment. What else should a good model do for us?**

2. **Suppose you have two eggs in the refrigerator. One is raw and the other is hard-boiled, but you do not know which is which. You spin each egg. One egg spins freely. The other egg comes to rest after very few rotations.**
    a. **Suggest a model that will account for the different behavior of the two eggs.**
    b. **On the basis of your model, what do you predict about the spinning of the two eggs after you boil both for 10 minutes?**
    c. **Check your prediction at home.**

 EXPERIMENT

8.2 Experiment: A Black Box

All the boxes you and your classmates will use in this experiment are the same (Figure 8.1). The first step is to find out as much as you can about these boxes without pulling out the rods, and, of course, without opening

Figure 8.1

A "black box."

the boxes. Look at one of them, shake it lightly, tilt it back and forth in various directions, and listen carefully to the sounds. Writing down your observations will help you compare notes with your classmates. You will then be ready to arrive jointly at a model, make predictions, and test them.

Do all the experiments you can think of, short of pulling out the rods or opening the box. Try to imagine in a general way what is inside the box that could account for your observations. This will be your model for the box. Do not be distracted by details. Do not, for example, try to name the objects inside the box; only describe them by the properties that you have found in your experiments. If you hear something sliding on one of the rods, it might be a washer or a ring. The important point is that it is something with a hole in it through which the rod passes.

After you and your classmates have made models that account for your observations, predict what will happen when you pull out a particular rod. Also predict how this will affect the results of the tests you performed earlier. (Be sure to write down your predictions so that you can check them.)

Now you or one of your classmates may remove this rod from one of the boxes. Leave all the rods in place in the other boxes. If what happens confirms your prediction, you can use one of the other boxes to test predictions about what would happen if another rod were pulled out first. If, however, your first prediction was not confirmed, modify your model before experimenting further. Continue this process until you have arrived at a model in which you have confidence.

3. While doing Experiment 8.2, A Black Box, why were you not permitted to open the box and look inside?

4. a. In investigating the black box, you did certain things to it that you could undo. Give some examples.
   b. What did you do to the black box that you could not undo?
   c. Does dissolving zinc in hydrochloric acid resemble any of the kinds of tests you mentioned in part (a) or part (b)?

5. In what way is pulling a rod from a black box similar to heating baking soda in Experiment 1.1?

8.3 The Atomic Model of Matter

Let us now begin to build an atomic model for matter by reviewing some of the common properties of elements, mixtures, and compounds. The assumptions we introduce into the model must account for these properties. Except in the last two sections of this chapter, we shall concentrate on stable, nonradioactive matter.

First, we consider elements. Different samples of an element have the same characteristic properties. To account for this, we shall assume that an element is made up of tiny particles of only one kind. We call these particles *atoms*. Different elements are made up of different kinds of atoms. Atoms cannot be seen even with strong microscopes. So they must be very small and there must be very many of them in any sample large enough for us to examine.

At this point we do not know how atoms of different elements differ from each other. But we can use familiar objects to illustrate the idea. Figure 8.2 shows a group of paper fasteners and a group of rubber rings. Think of a fastener as an atom of element Fs, and think of a ring as an atom of element R. Of course, nobody believes that an atom looks like a fastener or a ring. But this simple analogy illustrates the basic idea of the atomic model: All atoms of one element are alike, but they are different from the atoms of all other elements.

Figure 8.2
Paper fasteners representing atoms of "element" Fs, and rubber rings representing atoms of "element" R.

Second, we consider mixtures. Mixtures of elements can be made in varying proportions. Furthermore, the characteristic properties of a mixture can be made to vary widely by varying the amounts of the elements being mixed. And at least some of the characteristic properties of the individual elements (for example, color and the ability to react with other substances) are usually present in a mixture.

We can account for the behavior of mixtures by assuming that in mixtures the atoms of the individual elements remain unchanged. The numbers and masses of the atoms remain the same. The atoms just get mixed like marbles of different colors. Note that with this assumption the model guarantees that mass is conserved when mixtures are made and separated. Figure 8.3 provides a visualization of a mixture of two elements in terms of fasteners and rings.

Third, we consider compounds. When elements form compounds, they combine only in a definite ratio. You saw evidence for the law of constant proportions in the burning of hydrogen with oxygen (Section 6.3) and in the synthesis of zinc chloride (Experiment 6.4). Furthermore, the compound produced in each case had its own set of characteristic properties, usually quite different from those of the reacting elements. For example, the characteristic properties of carbon dioxide are entirely different from those of the carbon and oxygen that combine to make it.

Figure 8.3
Two mixtures of the "elements" Fs and R in very different proportions.

Figure 8.4

The compound FsR made by attaching one "atom" of Fs to one "atom" of R. Note the excess of Fs.

To account for the law of constant proportions, a new assumption must be added to the atomic model. We assume that when a compound is formed, each atom of one element attaches to a fixed number of atoms of the other elements in a particular pattern. A simple illustration of compound formation is provided by the attachment of one "atom" of Fs to one "atom" of R (Figure 8.4). Note that the excess of Fs did not "react." Thus the idea of attachment leads directly to the law of constant proportions.

6. **If several bins of different sizes were completely filled with the compound FsR, which of the following would be the same?**
   A. The number of rings in each bin
   B. The number of rings and fasteners in each bin
   C. The percent by mass of rings in each bin
   D. The percent by mass of fasteners in each bin

7. **Suppose that *M* atoms of mercury combine with *N* atoms of oxygen to form mercury oxide. Which of the following choices represents the total number of atoms of mercury oxide produced?**
   A. *M*
   B. *N*
   C. *M* + *N*
   D. 2*M* + *N*

8. **Suppose the mercury oxide produced in Question 7 is then decomposed by heating to form gaseous mercury and oxygen. Which of the following choices represents the numbers of atoms of mercury and oxygen you would expect to find?**
   A. *M* atoms of mercury and no atoms of oxygen
   B. No atoms of mercury and *N* atoms of oxygen
   C. *M* atoms of mercury and *N* atoms of oxygen
   D. 2*M* atoms of mercury and *N* atoms of oxygen

9. **Would your answer to Question 8 be different if you had condensed the gases to liquid mercury and liquid oxygen?**

"EXPERIMENT"

8.4 Constant Composition Using Fasteners and Rings

To illustrate what the atomic model says about the formation of compounds, you will use the "elements" Fs and R introduced in the preceding section. When you fit rings on fasteners as shown in Figure 8.4, the number of rings and the number of fasteners do not change. Hence the total mass does not change. The atomic model accounts for the conservation of mass.

Making a compound from these objects is similar to forming copper oxide from copper and oxygen (Experiment 6.6, A Reaction with Copper). In that experiment you worked with large numbers of invisible atoms. In this experiment you will illustrate the process by using many visible "atoms" to form a sample of a compound.

• What is the mass of all the Fs that you have?

Make as much of the "compound" FsR as your supply of "atoms" allows by putting one ring on each fastener (Figure 8.4). When we write "FsR", we mean a compound made up of one "atom" of Fs for each "atom" of R.

• What is the mass of the product you have synthesized?

If you have an excess of Fs, find its mass.

• How much Fs reacted with R?
• What is the ratio of the mass of R to the mass of product in your sample of the "compound"?

Compare your results with those of your classmates.

• Does the ratio of the mass of R to the mass of product depend on how big a sample you make?

- Does the model as illustrated by fasteners and rings agree with the law of constant proportions?
- Would the ratio have been the same if you had used heavier rings?

Suppose you "decomposed" your "compound" into pure Fs and R by taking the rings off the fasteners. You would get back all the "atoms" you started with.

- If you then measured the masses of the "elements" Fs and R, would the model agree with the law of conservation of mass?

Suppose the atoms of Fs and R combined in a ratio of one atom of Fs and two atoms of R. Such a compound would have the formula FsR_2 (Figure 8.5). The "$_2$" in the formula means that there are two atoms of R for every atom of Fs in the compound.

- If you decomposed this compound, would the mass ratio of R to FsR_2 be constant regardless of the size of the sample or the excess of R you had when forming it?
- If so, would the constant be the same as the mass ratio of R to FsR?

Figure 8.5
The compound FsR_2 made by attaching one "atom" of Fs to two "atoms" of R. Note the excess of R.

10. Based on this "experiment," does the law of constant proportions tell you how many atoms of chlorine combine with one atom of zinc in Experiment 6.4, The Synthesis of Zinc Chloride?

11. Why is "Experiment" in quotes in the title of Section 8.4?

12. Is the mass of a ring attached to a fastener the same as a ring that is not attached?

13. Which of the following aspects of the atomic model are addressed in Experiment 8.4?
    A. Atoms are very small.
    B. All atoms of a given element are alike.
    C. Atoms attach themselves to each other in a fixed mass ratio.

14. Does the "experiment" with rubber rings and paper fasteners give you any information about the shape of an atom?

15. Suppose that you had either extra fasteners or extra rings remaining in "Experiment" 8.4.
    a. What do these extra fasteners and rings represent?
    b. Relate your answer to part (a) to the class results of Experiment 6.4, The Synthesis of Zinc Chloride

16. In the synthesis of water described in Section 6.3, different volumes of hydrogen were mixed with a constant volume of oxygen. Then the mixture was ignited by a spark. In part (a), there was some oxygen left over; in part (b), nearly all the oxygen and the hydrogen reacted; and in part (c), some hydrogen was left over. Describe these results in terms of the atomic model of matter.

17. Suppose that element A can form a compound with element B but not with element C. Element B can form a compound with C. How can you use fasteners, rings, and washers to represent these elements?

18. Describe the synthesis of zinc chloride (Experiment 6.4, The Synthesis of Zinc Chloride) in terms of fasteners, rings, and washers. (Hint: Hydrochloric acid contains hydrogen and chlorine.)

8.5 Molecules

When two elements form a compound, their atoms attach themselves in one or more constant ratios. This is as far as we have come in terms of the atomic model. Let us now try to be more specific.

Figure 8.6 shows several possible arrangements for a compound containing equal numbers of atoms of two elements. In Figure 8.6(a) the atoms of the two elements are clearly paired off, with space between each pair. In Figure 8.6(b) the atoms form clusters of four, while in Figure 8.6(c) and (d) we can no longer distinguish groups or clusters that contain a fixed number of atoms. In Figure 8.6(c) there is no particular order to the atoms, whereas in Figure 8.6(d) the atoms are arranged in neat rows. Which of these pictures fits the arrangement of atoms in real compounds? To answer this question, we go back to what we already know about the behavior of matter in bulk.

Anybody who has ever used a bicycle pump knows that it is quite easy to compress air, that is, to reduce its volume. The same is true for all gases. But try to reduce the volume of a small crystal of sodium chloride

Figure 8.6

Possible attachments of the atoms of two elements in a compound that contains equal numbers of each kind of atom.

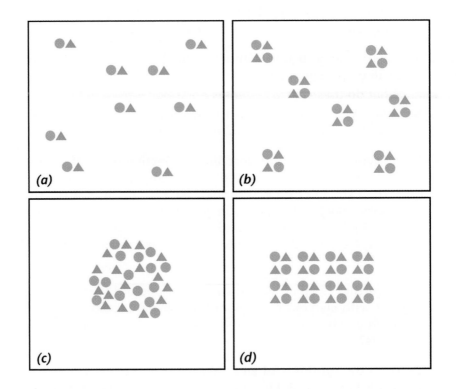

even by 1 percent. Without special equipment you will not succeed. A cube of copper will behave similarly.

While gases are quite compressible, solids are almost incompressible. We can account for this by assuming that atoms behave like little hard objects whose size remains fixed. In a solid, the atoms are close together; they are all "touching" one another. This means that the distance between the centers of the atoms equals the size of the atoms themselves (Figure 8.7). Such a picture suggests that solids are hard to compress. In

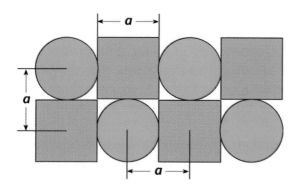

Figure 8.7

In a solid, the distance between the centers of adjacent atoms equals their size.

a gas, on the other hand, the atoms do not touch each other. They are far apart relative to their size; they can easily be pushed closer together to occupy a smaller volume (Figure 8.8).

A liquid or solid compound AB can be represented by Figure 8.6(c) or (d). A gas AB can be represented by Figure 8.6(a) or (b). Groups or clusters containing a fixed number of atoms are called *molecules*. Each molecule of a given compound contains the same number of atoms. (A substance with more than one kind of molecule is not a pure substance.)

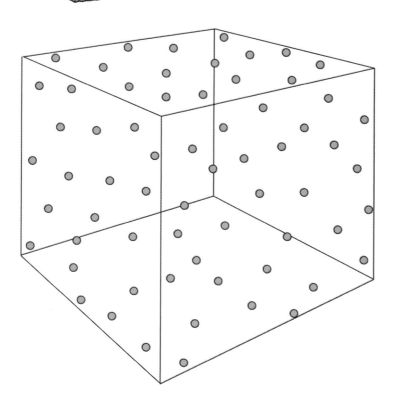

Figure 8.8

The large box represents a volume of helium gas at atmospheric pressure and room temperature. The spheres in the box represent helium atoms. The small box shows the volume occupied by the same helium atoms when helium is liquified.

Compounds are not the only substances made of molecules. The atoms of an element can also form clusters, or molecules, with only one kind of atom in each cluster. The analysis of many experiments and a long chain of arguments are necessary to determine the numbers of atoms in the molecules of different gases. In this course we do not present them. We shall simply state the results for some of the substances we have used as illustrations.

In gaseous hydrogen, the atoms cluster in pairs to form *diatomic* molecules. This is the reason why a molecule of hydrogen gas is written as H_2. The subscript indicates the number of atoms of a given element. The atoms of nitrogen and oxygen also cluster in pairs. A molecule of carbon dioxide (CO_2) is a cluster of two oxygen atoms and one carbon atom. The atoms of helium gas (He) and radon gas (Rn) do not form clusters. (Elements like these are said to have *monatomic* molecules.)

Every sample of a given compound contains the same elements in the same ratio by mass. However, two substances that have the same elements in the same ratio by mass need not be the same compound. For example, the two oxides of nitrogen, NO_2 and N_2O_4, have the same ratio of nitrogen and oxygen. However, the molecules of NO_2 have three atoms, and those of N_2O_4 have six atoms.

Another example is provided by ethyne (also called acetylene) and benzene, two compounds of carbon and hydrogen with the same mass ratio. A molecule of ethyne, C_2H_2, has four atoms. A molecule of benzene, C_6H_6, has twelve atoms. The two compounds have very different properties.

When atoms are arranged as in Figure 8.6(d), it is meaningless to talk about clusters or molecules. Describing such a solid as a compound AB tells us only that it contains equal numbers of the two kinds of atoms. Thus, the formula NaCl, when applied to solid sodium chloride, means only that the crystal contains equal numbers of sodium atoms and chlorine atoms. Similarly, the formula H_2O applied to water states only the ratio of hydrogen and oxygen atoms in the liquid. However, a molecule of water vapor is accurately described by H_2O.

19. Gold is a soft metal. With a hammer, a cube of gold can be pounded into a thin strip. Based on the atomic model, do you expect the volume of the strip to be different from the volume of the cube?

20. Draw diagrams similar to Figure 8.6 for nitrogen gas and for helium gas.

21. Suppose that you find two solid compounds, one more compressible than the other. Which compound do you think is better described by Figure 8.6(c) and which by Figure 8.6(d)?

EXPERIMENT

8.6 Flame Tests of Some Elements

As you saw in Chapter 6, some compounds are hard to break up into their elements. However, by holding small samples in a flame, even such compounds can be made to reveal the elements they contain.

Place small quantities of different compounds, each of which contains sodium, on tiny loops of nichrome wire and hold them in a flame. Record the color you see for each of the compounds.

Next, try the same experiment using copper and compounds containing copper. Repeat the same procedure with compounds containing strontium, lithium, and calcium.

- How can you recognize sodium in a compound by doing such a flame test?
- How can you recognize copper?
- Can you distinguish among strontium, lithium, and calcium by a flame test?

Although the characteristic properties of compounds are different from those of the elements that make them up, the color of the flame is due to the elements. We can understand the appearance of the colors in terms of the atomic model in the following way: The flame is not hot enough to break up the entire sample. But it can shake off some atoms from their compounds. Once these atoms are separated, they emit light of a color specific to them. It does not matter anymore from what compound they were released.

22. When you hold a small amount of sodium chloride in a flame, you observe that the flame is bright yellow. What can you do to be sure that the color is due to sodium and not to chlorine?

23. When you spill a few drops of soup or milk on a pale-blue gas flame when cooking, the color of the flame changes to a mixture of colors. Yellow is the most intense color. What do you conclude from this observation?

24. A product containing the compound copper sulfate can be sprinkled on a wood fire to add color to the flame. What color can you expect this compound to add?

EXPERIMENT
8.7 Spectra of Some Elements

As you probably just found out, some elements are easy to identify by a flame test. Many other elements are not so easily identified. For such elements we need to separate the mixed colors in order to detect slight differences. The first step is to spread out the various colors in the light in much the same way they appear in a rainbow. This spread of colors is called a *spectrum* (plural: *spectra*).

You can produce a spectrum using a simple grating spectroscope. This devise consists of a tube with a slit at one end and a transparent plastic disk at the other. The disk has many parallel lines on it.

Hold the end with the plastic grating next to your eye and look at several light sources provided by your teacher. When the light source is a thin tube, you may find it more convenient to look at the light with the slit removed.

- What is the major difference between the spectrum of an ordinary light bulb and the spectrum of any of the gas tubes?
- What are the differences between the spectra of the different gas tubes?

8.8 Spectral Analysis

We mentioned compounds of calcium, lithium, and strontium without specifying which compound we were talking about. This may give you the impression that the spectrum of only one of the elements in a compound can be observed. This is not so. The flame of your burner is hot enough to produce the spectra of sodium, lithium, calcium, copper, and a few other elements. It is not hot enough to produce the spectra of elements such as oxygen and chlorine. However, the very high temperatures generated by an electric arc will produce the spectra of all the elements in a compound.

Under such conditions the resulting spectrum is no longer simple. It will most likely contain complicated patterns of many closely spaced lines. Yet each element gives out its own spectrum, which is different from that of any other element. It takes accurate measurements of the positions of spectral lines to identify an element. Once this has been done, the presence of any element has been definitely established.

With a good instrument, the sodium spectrum looks like Figure 8.9. This shows that the yellow of the sodium flame is not just any yellow. It is a very specific color indeed, which has its own place in the spectrum. No other element has a line at this place in the spectrum. The presence of this particular pair of lines always means that sodium is present in the

(a)

(b)

Figure 8.9

(a) The spectrum of sodium. The spectrum was in black and white; the color was added later. Therefore, the positions of the lines are accurate, but their colors are not. The line in the yellow is extremely intense. It has been photographed through an absorbing filter so it can be seen at the same time as the other lines. The almost invisible violet line arises from a potassium impurity. (b) A part of the sodium spectrum has been photographed with a spectroscope that spreads out the light more, enabling us to see more detail. Now we can see that the yellow line is actually made up of two lines that are very close together.

light source. Even if the yellow color in the flame is masked by many other colors, the spectroscope will reveal the presence of sodium.

Figure 8.10 illustrates spectra obtained from compounds of calcium, lithium, and strontium. All these elements give flame tests of nearly the same color. However, each has its own set of characteristic spectral lines when viewed through a spectroscope.

Calcium

Lithium

Strontium

Figure 8.10

The brightest lines in the spectra of calcium, lithium, and strontium.

Figure 8.11

A comparison between the spectrum of pure helium (upper half) and the spectrum produced in an evacuated tube containing polonium (lower half). The two faint lines close together in the lower half are polonium lines.

Unlike the measurement of melting point or density, spectral analysis, or spectroscopy, can be done on very distant objects like our sun and other stars. Analysis of sunlight was one of the very early uses of spectroscopy. Most of the spectral lines observed in sunlight could also be produced with known materials in the laboratory. However, during a solar eclipse in 1868, a new set of spectral lines was found in the spectrum of the light coming from the edge of the sun. This set of lines had never been seen before, and could not be produced in the laboratory with any element known at the time. The lines were therefore thought to be from a new element, which was named "helium" after the Greek word for sun. Eventually, helium was also detected on Earth through spectral analysis.

In Section 7.2 we mentioned that the elements produced in the radioactive decomposition of polonium were identified by spectral analysis. The formation of helium in this process was demonstrated for use in this course by the following procedure:

The upper half of Figure 8.11 shows the spectrum of helium contained in a tube like one you may have seen in the classroom. The lower half shows the spectrum obtained from a tube that was prepared this way: 4.5×10^{-3} g of polonium was deposited inside, the air was pumped out, and the tube was sealed. Thirteen days after this the spectrum was photographed.

Note that the three lines in the upper half of Figure 8.11 appear at the same positions in the lower half. The exposure was weaker in the lower half (the lines are thinner); this is why the line near the middle is barely visible in the lower half. The mass of the helium in this experiment is calculated in Section 9.4 and found to be 6.8×10^{-6} g, less than seven millionths of a gram!

The usefulness of spectroscopy in recognizing minute quantities of an element is not new. During the first few years of spectroscopy, five elements that are present on Earth in only tiny concentrations were discovered. For example, the spectrum of minerals found in the water of a certain spring in Germany was analyzed. Two lines of unknown origin were found in the blue region of the spectrum. This bit of evidence was enough to challenge Robert Bunsen, a German chemist, to search for a new element in the water. He evaporated 40,000 kg of spring water to isolate a sample of the new element, which he named "cesium."

In Chapters 5 and 6 you used the characteristic properties of bulk matter to determine the composition of substances. In spectroscopy the properties of atoms are used for the same purpose. The results of the two methods always agree completely.

25. Figure A shows some spectra observed with the same spectroscope that was used for Figure 8.10. Which elements can you identify in part (a)? in part (b)?

Figure A
For problem 25

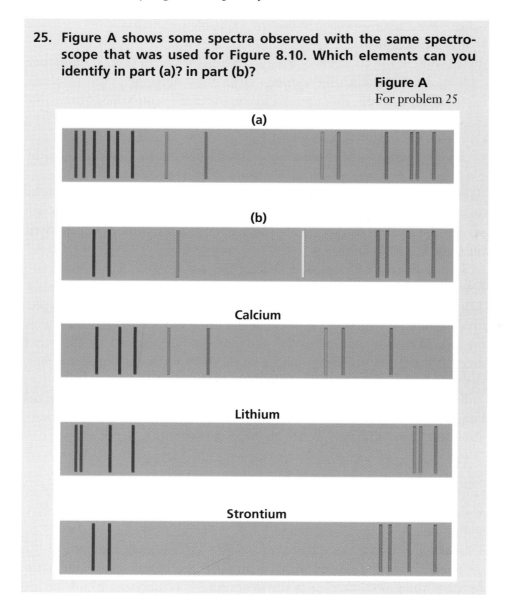

(a)

(b)

Calcium

Lithium

Strontium

26. **Suppose a compound composed of three elements is known to contain sodium and oxygen. Describe how to use spectral analysis to identify the third element.**

"EXPERIMENT"

8.9 An Analog for Radioactive Decay

Having been motivated by radioactivity to develop an atomic model of matter, we are now ready to expand the model with additional assumptions. These assumptions will lead to a testable prediction.

We shall assume that:

(i) Whenever an atom of a radioactive element decays, it emits one particle, which affects a counter or other detector.

(ii) This process takes place by chance: all atoms have the same chance to decay in any time interval. There is no way of telling which atom will decay next.

(iii) The chance for the decay of a particular atom is not affected by whether other atoms have or have not already decayed.

From these assumptions some startling conclusions can be drawn by using the power of mathematics. We shall not do that. Instead, you will act out the process as directed by the assumptions, as you did in the synthesis of FsR in Section 8.4.

The radioactive atoms will be represented by dice. Each team will begin with 12 dice. The dice will be shaken and thrown on the table. The dice that land with a six on top will be considered to have decayed. Shaking the dice gives each of them the same chance to land with a six on top. Also, how any particular die lands is not affected by the other dice. By carefully watching for the sixes, you will be the counter. Thus, the dice analog satisfies the assumptions of the model.

Each throw stands for some fixed time interval. A record of the number of dice that decay and that remain will illustrate what the model says about the decay of a radioactive element over time.

- Why should you remove the dice with a six on top before you throw the dice again?

- Why should you thoroughly shake the remaining dice before the next throw?

Shake and throw the dice ten times. Be sure to keep a record of the number of dice you started with, the number that decayed, and the number that remained after each throw. Figure 8.12 shows a graph of the

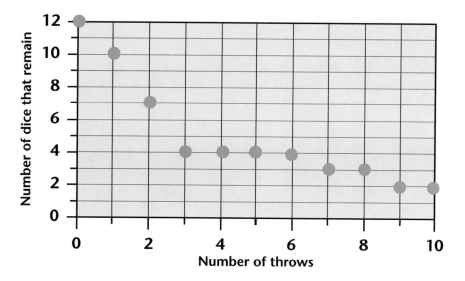

Figure 8.12

A graph of the number of remaining dice as a function of the number of throws.

number of remaining dice as a function of the number of throws for one run. Draw a graph like Figure 8.12 from your data.

- Is your graph exactly the same as Figure 8.12? Does your graph look exactly like any of the graphs of the teams near you?

A radioactive source producing a small number of counts per minute is considered a weak source. A set of 12 dice is a model for a very weak radioactive source. To see how a strong radioactive source would act, you can add the decay data from the entire class. Now you can draw a smooth curve that passes quite close to the class data.

- How many throws did it take for the number of remaining dice to reach half the original value?
- In how many throws did the number of remaining dice drop from half the original value to one quarter of the original value?

With dice, you can count both the decaying and the remaining ones. With a real radioactive element, you can measure only the number of atoms decaying per unit time, that is, the decay rate. To draw testable conclusions from the model, you must relate the graph of remaining dice to a graph of the decay rate.

We assumed that the chance of an atom to decay is independent of how many atoms are in the sample. Therefore, we expect that the greater the number of atoms in a sample, the greater the decay rate. By the same reasoning, a sample with half the number of atoms would have half the decay rate.

- What do you conclude from the preceding paragraph about the shape of a graph of decay rate as a function of the number of throws?
- Does your answer to the preceding question remind you of any graphs in Chapter 7? If so, which and why?

27. **Of the following choices, which describes how the probability that an atom of a radioactive element will decay during a 10-minute interval a year from now compares with the probability that it will decay in the next 10 minutes?**
    A. greater
    B. the same
    C. smaller

28. **Suppose your class used a large number of pennies instead of dice and removed those pennies displaying "heads" after each toss.**
    a. **How many tosses would it take for the number of pennies remaining to reach one-half the original number of pennies?**
    b. **How many tosses would be required to reduce the number of pennies to one-fourth of the original number?**

29. **Recall the assumptions of the model for radioactive decay. Explain in your own words how these assumptions are satisfied by the dice analog.**

30. a. **Is it possible to roll 6 dice and have more display a six than if 12 dice were rolled?**
    b. **Is it more probable to roll a six if 12 dice or 6 dice are rolled?**

8.10 Half-Life

The throwing of dice cannot tell us how much time it will take the decay rate of a radioactive element to drop to half its initial value. But the model makes the following prediction for any radioactive element: Whatever time it takes to reduce the decay rate to one half its initial value, it will take the *same* time to reduce it from one half to one quarter of the initial value. It will take the same time to reduce the decay rate from one quarter to one eighth, and so on.

Thus, every radioactive element has a *half-life*, that is, a time during which its decay rate reduces to half its initial value. This half-life is a characteristic property of the element; it is independent of the number of atoms in the sample.

The counting rate measured with a Geiger counter does not equal the decay rate because not all particles enter the counter; some are emitted in other directions. But if we keep the counter always at the same distance from the sample, then the counting rate will be proportional to the decay rate. This prediction can, and has been, tested. All radioactive elements have a half-life. The values of the half-lives for a few elements are given in Table 8.1.

Table 8.1

Element	Half-life	Element	Half-life
Uranium	4.5×10^9 years	Polonium	138 days
Radium	1.6×10^3 years	Radon	3.83 days

31. Consider the two quantities, *half-life* and *decay rate*.
    a. Which, if either, of these two quantities depends only on the kind of element?
    b. Which, if either, depends also on the number of atoms in the sample?

32. Suppose that at a particular moment, you have two samples, one of radon and one of polonium. Each sample contains a billion (1×10^9) atoms.
    a. After 3.83 days, which sample will contain more of the original atoms?
    b. Were there more decays of polonium atoms or of radon atoms during this period?
    c. Which of the two samples has a higher decay rate?
    d. Under the same conditions, which sample will show a greater counting rate?

33. Suppose you repeat "Experiment" 8.9, An Analog for Radioactive Decay, with the following change: A die showing a five or a three on each throw shall be considered to have decayed.
    a. Will the dice still show a half-life? Why?
    b. If your answer to part (a) was "yes," how will the new half-life relate to the one you observed in Experiment 8.9? Try it, if you wish.

34. Think again of the sealed can referred to in Section 8.1. You are not allowed to pierce the can or break it open. What would you predict about its behavior in each case?

    a. You lowered the temperature sufficiently.

    b. You raised the temperature sufficiently.

35. Consider the following activities:

    A. Determining the density of water

    B. Dissolving salt in water

    C. Measuring the freezing point of a liquid

    D. Dissolving an Alka-Seltzer tablet in water

    E. Heating baking soda

    Which of these activities are analogous to shaking the black box, and which are analogous to pulling out a rod?

36. Which of the following are *parts* of the atomic model of matter, and which are *illustrations* of the model?

    A. Matter is made up of very tiny particles.

    B. Atoms of the same element are all alike.

    C. A rubber ring combines with a fastener to form FsR.

    D. Atoms of different elements may combine to form compounds.

    E. Marbles can be stacked in a box to represent a solid.

37. In the nineteenth century, Louis Pasteur developed a "germ model" for disease. According to Pasteur, little organisms, too small to be seen by the unaided eye, were the cause of disease.

    a. How does this model account for the fact that people get sick?

    b. What predictions does the model make about staying healthy?

    c. What are some of the limitations of this model? (Hint: Think of kidney stones or heart attacks.)

38. Suppose that 6 million atoms of hydrogen combine with 2 million atoms of nitrogen to form 2 million molecules of ammonia. How many atoms of hydrogen and how many atoms of nitrogen will there be in each molecule of ammonia?

39. How deep would 40,000 kg of water (the amount evaporated by Robert Bunsen to discover cesium) stand in your classroom?

40. Refer to the graph of the number of remaining dice as a function of the number of throws (Figure 8.12).

   a. How many throws are needed to reduce the initial number of dice to 80%?

   b. How many throws are needed to reduce the initial number of dice to 80% of 80%, that is, to 64%?

   c. How many throws are needed to reduce the initial number to 80% of 80% of 80%, that is, 51%?

   d. Is "the time in which 80% of the number of atoms of a radioactive element remain" a characteristic property of the element? If yes, how is this time related to the half-life?

41. Many radioactive elements are waste products in nuclear power plants. Periodically, this waste must be removed and stored in a safe place. Suppose that three radioactive elements are produced. Suppose their half-lives are 30 minutes, 500 years, and 1×10^8 years. Suppose also that when the waste is ready to be shipped, the three elements are present in equal numbers of atoms.

   a. Which of the three elements will have the highest decay rate?

   b. The atoms of which of the three elements will still be present in significant numbers after one year?

   c. If not stored safely, which of the remaining elements will pose a health hazard after 100 years?

42. a. Since polonium has a half-life of 138 days, it must itself be a product of radioactive decomposition of another element. Why?

   b. Will a freshly prepared sample of polonium have the same half-life as the remainder of an old sample?

THEME FOR A SHORT ESSAY

In or around your house, there are devices that perform particular tasks. You know how to use these devices but you do not know how they work. For you, such devices are "black boxes." Choose one of these devices, describe in detail what it does when you operate it, and explain why it is a "black box" to you.

9 Sizes and Masses of Molecules an Atoms

Molecules and atoms are not visible even under powerful optical microscopes. How, then, can you answer any of the following questions: How big is an atom? What is the mass of one atom? How many atoms are in a sample of matter that you can work with in the laboratory? These three questions are related. If you can measure any one of these quantities, you can calculate the others. You will do just that in this chapter. However, you will use indirect methods. The first method is introduced in the section below.

9.1 The Thickness of a Thin Layer

Consider a rectangular solid. Its volume V is equal to its length times its width times its height, or $V = lwh$ [Figure 9.1(a)]. Since lw is the area of the base, we can say that the volume equals the area of the base times the height.

Figure 9.1(b) shows another rectangular solid with the same volume as that in Figure 9.1(a). The material has been formed into a different rectangular shape that has a larger base and a much smaller height. Its volume is still the area of its base times its height. If the material were spread out into an even thinner layer, its volume would be unchanged and would still be equal to the area of its base times its height.

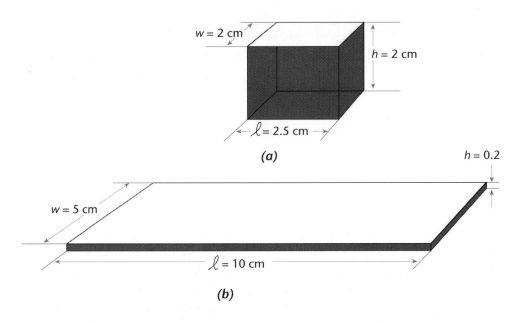

(a)

(b)

Figure 9.1

The piece of matter in (a) has a volume of lwh = 2.5 cm × 2.0 cm × 2.0 cm = 10 cm³. In (b) the same piece of matter has been flattened. It has the same volume as in (a). The volume of the thin slab in (b) is lwh = 10 cm × 5 cm × 0.2 cm = 10 cm³.

Now suppose you have a thin rectangular sheet of some material—a metal foil, for example—whose volume you know. From measurements of its length and width, you can calculate the area of its base. To find the thickness, you divide the known volume by the area of the base.

The same method works for a circular sheet. The volume of a circular sheet is also equal to the area of the base times the height. In the case of a circular sheet, or cylinder, the base area is equal to πr^2, where r is the radius of the base. You will apply this method to both rectangular and circular objects later in this chapter.

---

1. **A rectangular solid has length of 10.0 cm, a width of 5.0 cm, and a volume of 10.0 cm³. Which of the following is the thickness of the solid in cm?**

   A. 0.2

   B. 2.0

   C. 500

2. **A circular solid (cylinder) has a diameter of 20 cm and a volume of 30 cm³. What is the height of the cylinder?**

EXPERIMENT

9.2 The Thickness of a Thin Sheet of Metal

You can find the thickness of a rectangular sheet of aluminum foil from its length, width, and volume. To find the volume you need to know the mass of the sheet and the density of the material (2.7 g/cm³).

- From your calculation of the foil's thickness, how thick can the atoms of aluminum be?

- How thin can they be?

Metals do not flatten out into thin layers by themselves; they have to be rolled or hammered. Hammering, however, is a crude process. Even the most skilled goldsmith, making thin gold leaf for lettering on store windows, must stop when the gold leaf is about 10^{-5} cm thick. In such cases, the minimum thickness is determined not by the size of the fundamental particles of gold but by the difficulty of handling such a thin sheet.

Liquids, on the other hand, tend to spread out into thin layers by themselves. If you pour water on the floor, it spreads out quickly to form a thin layer. You can calculate the thickness of this layer if you know the volume of the water you pour out and the area it covers.

In the next experiment, you will use a liquid that spreads out even more thinly than water. To calculate such a small thickness, it would be convenient to express the numbers in *scientific notation*. If you are not familiar with scientific notation, you may find it helpful to study the Appendix on page 203.

3. In a small-boat harbor, a careless sailor dumps overboard a quart (about 1,000 cm³) of diesel oil. Assume that this oil will spread evenly over the surface of the water to a thickness of 0.00010 cm. What area will be covered with oil?

4. A tiny drop of mercury has a volume of 0.0010 cm³. The density of mercury is about 14 g/cm³. What is the mass of the drop?

5. A goldsmith hammers 19.3 g of gold into a thin sheet of foil that is 100 cm in length and 100 cm in width. The density of gold is 19.3 g/cm³.
   a. What is the volume of the gold?
   b. What is the area of the gold sheet?
   c. What is the thickness of the gold sheet?

6. The following measurements were recorded for a rectangular slab of aluminum. (The density of aluminum is 2.7 g/cm³.)

Length	7.60 cm
Width	2.50 cm
Mass	30.78 g

What is the height of the aluminum slab?

EXPERIMENT

9.3 The Size and Mass of an Oleic Acid Molecule

You are now ready to calculate the size and the mass of a single molecule. The starting point will be finding the thickness of a very thin layer of a substance. To do that, you will follow the same approach that you used in Experiment 9.2, The Thickness of a Thin Sheet of Metal.

Under proper conditions, oil and certain other substances can spread out even more thinly than water. Oil does not dissolve in water, it floats on top of it. You often see oil spread out on a water surface in a thin, rainbow-colored film. Oleic acid, a compound of hydrogen, carbon, and oxygen, does not dissolve in water either but spreads out into an even thinner layer than oil does. In fact, a single drop of this liquid from a medicine dropper will spread so thin that it will cover the entire surface of a small wading pool.

To make it possible to do the experiment in a small tray, we must dilute the solution of oleic acid in alcohol. In this experiment you will be using a solution that is 1 part oleic acid in 500 parts of solution, or 2×10^{-3} parts of oleic acid.

Pour tap water into a tray to a depth of about half a centimeter. Allow the water to stand for a few minutes, until all movement has stopped. Then sprinkle just enough fine powder on the water to make a barely visible layer. When a drop of dilute solution of oleic acid is dropped onto the water surface, the powder will be pushed aside. This allows you to see the oleic acid film when it spreads out across the water (Figure 9.2).

To prove that it is the oleic acid and not the alcohol that pushes the powder aside, first put one drop of pure alcohol from a medicine dropper in the center of the tray.

- What do you observe?

Now put one drop of the dilute solution in the center of the tray.

- If the area covered by the film is very nearly circular, what is the diameter of the circle?
- If the area is only roughly circular, how will you find its average diameter?
- What is the area of the thin film?

(a)   **(b)**

Figure 9.2

A close-up of the tray with motionless water. (a) After a thin layer of powder has been sprinkled on the water. (b) After a drop of dilute solution of oleic acid has been dropped from a medicine dropper.

To find the volume of the acid in the thin layer, you must first find the volume of one drop of the dilute solution. You can do that by counting the number of drops that will add up to 1.0 cm³ in a graduated cylinder.

- What is the volume of one drop of solution?
- What is the volume of oleic acid in one drop of the solution? (Remember that only 1/500 of the solution is oleic acid.)
- From your volume and area measurements, what is the thickness of the layer?

So far you have found only the height of a molecule of oleic acid. Other experiments show that oleic acid molecules are long and thin, with a height about 10 times the width of their base. They stand nearly upright on a water surface when they form a thin layer. Thus a tiny piece of a layer of oleic acid one molecule thick might look roughly like the collection of tiny rods in Figure 9.3. The area of the base of each rod is then equal to the width of the base squared, as shown in Figure 9.4.

Suppose that all the molecules of oleic acid touch one another, as in Figure 9.3.

Figure 9.3

A simplified picture of a submicroscopic piece of a film of oleic acid one molecule thick.

Then,

Area of layer = (number of molecules) . (base area of one molecule)

or,

$$\text{Number of molecules} = \frac{\text{area of layer}}{\text{base area of one molecule}}$$

- From your data for the height of one molecule and the fact that the width is about 1/10 of the height, what is the area of the base of one molecule?
- What is the number of molecules in the layer?
- What does this tell you about the number of molecules in the droplet you started with?

From the volume of the oleic acid in one drop of dilute solution and the density of oleic acid, you can calculate the mass of oleic acid in one drop of dilute solution. The density of oleic acid is 0.87 g/cm³. Since this is a very rough calculation, you may substitute 1 g/cm³ for the density of oleic acid.

- What is the mass of the droplet of oleic acid?

Knowing the number of molecules in the droplet, you can now use the relation

$$\text{Mass of one molecule} = \frac{\text{mass of sample}}{\text{number of molecules in sample}}$$

to find the mass of a single molecule of oleic acid.

- What is the mass of one molecule of oleic acid?

Figure 9.4
Enlarged view of a simplified picture of a single oleic acid molecule. The area of the base (the darker region) is equal to (width)².

7. Can the height of a single molecule of oleic acid be greater than the thickness of the layer of oleic acid?

8. Can the size of an atom of hydrogen, carbon, or oxygen be greater than the width of an oleic acid molecule?

9. Suppose the mass of 1.3×10^{18} molecules of oleic acid is 3.8×10^5 g. Of the following choices, which shows the calculation you can use to find the mass of one molecule of oleic acid?

   A. $\dfrac{1.3 \times 10^{18}}{3.8 \times 10^5}$ B. $\dfrac{3.8 \times 10^5}{1.3 \times 10^{18}}$ C. $1.3 \times 10^{18} \times 3.8 \times 10^5$

9.4 The Mass of Helium Atoms

By indirect but simple means, you were able to determine the mass of a
single molecule of oleic acid. Now we shall describe an experiment in
which the mass of a single helium atom is found. The experiment was
done for *IPS* students at the Mound Laboratory of the Monsanto
Research Corporation. This experiment is shown in the film, "The Mass
of Atoms." Figures 9.5 through 9.7 and Figure 9.10 are from the film.

As in your experiment with oleic acid, an indirect method was used.
The main idea of the experiment was to prepare a sample of helium of
known mass and known number of atoms. The mass of a single atom
was then calculated by division:

$$\text{Mass of atom} = \frac{\text{mass of sample}}{\text{number of atoms in sample}}$$

The helium was produced by the radioactive decay of polonium. A
small amount of polonium was placed inside a quartz tube of known
diameter. The air was pumped out and the tube was sealed (Figure 9.5).

Figure 9.5

The sealed quartz tube containing polonium. The polonium produces
a blue glow, caused by the emitted helium particles when they strike
the quartz. This photograph was taken in the light from the blue glow.

After 21 days the seal was broken underwater. The water rushed into the tube and compressed the helium to atmospheric pressure (see Figure 9.6). From the volume of the helium and its known density at atmospheric pressure, the mass of the helium sample was calculated. The number of helium atoms was calculated from the average counting rate per minute and the number of minutes in 21 days.

Figure 9.6
The quartz tube containing helium after being opened underwater.
The length of the gas column is 5.0 cm.

In principle, the polonium could now be removed from the tube and placed in a counter in order to find the number of disintegrations per minute. However, in practice this is not possible. A sample large enough to produce a measurable amount of helium in three weeks would give off too many helium particles per minute for the counter to count. Therefore, the polonium was first dissolved completely in a large quantity of nitric acid. The solution was further diluted with water. In both steps, the solution was thoroughly mixed to make sure the polonium was evenly distributed throughout. Finally, a tiny drop of the solution was put on a small plate, the acid was evaporated, and the plate placed in a counter (Figure 9.7).

Figure 9.7
A metal plate containing polonium being removed from a radiation counter after a count.

Here is the record of the data of the experiment:

Production of Helium

On March 3 the polonium was sealed in the evacuated quartz tube. The seal was broken on March 24. The water rose in the tube and the helium was compressed to a length of 5.0 cm in the tube (Figure 9.6).

The area of the cross section of the inside of the quartz tube, checked beforehand, was 8.1×10^{-3} cm². Thus the volume of helium in the tube was

$$\begin{aligned} \text{Volume} &= \text{length} \cdot \text{area of cross section} \\ &= 5.0 \text{ cm} \times 8.1 \times 10^{-3} \text{ cm}^2 \\ &= 4.1 \times 10^{-2} \text{ cm}^3. \end{aligned}$$

The density of helium at atmospheric pressure and room temperature is 1.7×10^{-4} g/cm³. The mass of the sample of helium is

$$\begin{aligned} \text{Mass} &= \text{volume} \cdot \text{density} \\ &= 4.1 \times 10^{-2} \text{ cm}^3 \times 1.7 \times 10^{-4} \text{ g/cm}^3 \\ &= 7.0 \times 10^{-6} \text{ g}. \end{aligned}$$

Dilution

The small sample of polonium was first dissolved in 1.0×10^3 cm³ of nitric acid. Therefore, one cubic centimeter of this solution contains 1/1,000 of the original amount of polonium.

A volume of 1.0 cm³ of this solution was then mixed with 99 cm³ of water. Hence 1.0 cm³ of this dilute solution contained only 1 part in 10^5 (or 1.0×10^{-5}) of the original sample of polonium. Even this was too much to be counted!

Therefore, only 1.0×10^{-3} cm³ (one one-thousandth of a cubic centimeter) of the very dilute polonium solution was placed on the plate to be counted. This meant that only

$$1.0 \times 10^{-5} \times 1.0 \times 10^{-3} = 1.0 \times 10^{-8},$$

or 1 part in 100 million, of the original polonium was counted. Two trials were run with samples of this size.

Counting

Trial 1: 2.4×10^5 counts/minute

Trial 2: 2.0×10^5 counts/minute

This step introduces the largest experimental error on the experiment so far. The average of the two readings, 2.2×10^5 counts/minute, was used.

The counter used in the experiment described above does not count those helium particles that fly off into the plate; it counts only those that fly off upward (Figure 9.8). Thus the true disintegration rate was twice the recorded number, 4.4×10^5 counts/minute.

Figure 9.8

Helium particles flying off from a thin polonium source *S* on a metal plate. Those emitted in the directions shown by the arrows can be counted. Half of the helium particles are emitted downward into the plate and are not counted.

This large number of counts is produced by only 1.0×10^{-8} of the original sample. The number of disintegrations per minute of the whole sample is

$1.0 \times 10^8 \times 4.4 \times 10^5$ counts/min = 4.4×10^{13} counts/min.

Now recall that the quartz tube containing the polonium was sealed on March 3 and opened on March 24. This is a period of 21 days or

21 days $\times$ 24 hours/day $\times$ 60 min/hour = 3.0×10^4 min.

If the sample of polonium had decayed at the same rate over the entire duration of the experiment, then the total number of counts would have been

4.4×10^{13} counts/min $\times$ 3.0×10^4 min = 1.3×10^{18} counts.

Of course, the counting rate is not constant; it decreases with time. Like all radioactive elements, polonium has a half-life (Section 8.10). Specifically, the half-life of polonium is 138 days (see Figure 9.9). After 21 days the rate of decay is 0.90 of the original rate. So the average rate

Figure 9.9

The rate of decay of a sample containing polonium as a function of time. The rate (number of polonium atoms that disintegrate per unit time) is expressed in terms of the fraction of the rate measured at zero days. The rate reaches 0.5 of the original value at 138 days, the half-life of polonium.

of decay over the first 21 days is about 0.95 of the original rate. Thus the counting rate measured after 21 days must be divided by 0.95 to give the average counting rate over the 21 days. This correction will raise the total number of counts during the experiment to about 1.4×10^{18}.

Therefore, we shall use the value 1.4×10^{18} for the total number of counts during the experiment.

We said earlier that we shall assume that each decay signals the formation of one helium atom. Thus the number of helium atoms produced by the polonium sample during the three weeks is:

$$\text{Number of helium atoms} = 1.4 \times 10^{18}$$

and the mass of one helium atom is

$$\text{Mass of atom} = \frac{\text{mass of sample}}{\text{number of atoms in sample}}$$

$$= \frac{7.0 \times 10^{-6} \text{ g}}{1.4 \times 10^{18}} = 5.0 \times 10^{-24} \text{ g}$$

12. If the mass of an atom of an element is 5.0×10^{-23} g, how many atoms are there in 1 g of that element?

13. A cylindrical tube with a cross-sectional area of 2 cm² and a height of 50 cm is filled with hydrogen. What is the volume of the hydrogen in the tube?

14. Write a brief summary of the steps followed in finding the mass of helium atoms by radioactive decay.

15. In the experiment on the mass of helium, how many lead atoms were formed? What assumptions are made to get this number?

9.5 The Mass of Polonium Atoms

We can apply the relation

$$\text{Mass of atom} = \frac{\text{mass of sample}}{\text{number of atoms in sample}}$$

to polonium as well as to helium. We assumed that one atom of polonium disintegrates into one atom of lead and one atom of helium. Therefore, the number of atoms of polonium that disintegrated during the three weeks of the experiment equals the number of helium atoms formed. This number we calculated in the preceding section. To calculate the mass of one polonium atom, we must know the mass of the polonium that disintegrated.

As we saw in the preceding section, the rate of decay of polonium after 21 days is 0.90, or 90%, of the original rate. Since the rate of decay is proportional to the number of polonium atoms present, 0.90 of the original mass of polonium remained in the quartz tube. In other words, 0.10 of the initial sample had decayed.

All this we learn from Figure 9.9. But to find out how much polonium decayed, you have to know the initial mass of the polonium. Although we did not mention it before, the polonium was massed before it was placed in the quartz tube (Figure 9.10).

Massing polonium is difficult. Because of the intense and dangerous radiation, the polonium must be massed inside a small closed container. The procedure resembles the massing of a liquid. Here we state only the final result, found by massing the container plus polonium, then subtracting the mass of the container.

$$\text{Mass of polonium sample} = 4.5 \times 10^{-3} \text{ g}$$

$$\text{Mass of polonium that decayed} = 0.10 \times 4.5 \times 10^{-3} \text{ g}$$

$$= 4.5 \times 10^{-4} \text{ g}$$

$$\text{Number of atoms of polonium that decayed} = 1.4 \times 10^{18}$$

$$\text{Mass of one polonium atom} = \frac{4.5 \times 10^{-4}}{1.4 \times 10^{18}} = 3.2 \times 10^{-22} \text{ g}$$

$$= 320 \times 10^{-24} \text{ g}$$

We wrote the mass of a polonium atom to the same power of ten as for the mass of a helium atom. We see that polonium atoms are about 320/5.0 = 64 times as heavy as helium atoms.

The two experiments involve the determination of the mass and number of atoms in a small sample. They are by no means the first or the most accurate of such determinations, but they are perhaps the most direct. A repetition of this experiment, which you may see in the film, "The Mass of Atoms,"

Figure 9.10

A few milligrams of polonium being weighed on a sensitive balance. The polonium is in a small glass tube in the sealed bottle on the left-hand pan. The bottle is sealed to prevent contamination of the balance and the laboratory by the polonium.

gave a similar result: 7.5×10^{-24} g for helium and 410×10^{-24} g for polonium. For higher precision, different methods are used and give a mass of 6.64×10^{-24} g for helium and 349×10^{-24} g for polonium.

Before studying this experiment, you had no way of guessing what the mass of a single atom might be. The mass might have been a billion times larger than 10^{-24} g—that is, about 10^{-15} g—or perhaps 10^{-33} g, a billion times smaller. Thus, being able to conclude that the mass of a helium atom is close to 6×10^{-24} g is an impressive achievement.

Although the masses of atoms vary over a wide range, they are all very small compared with the masses you are likely to put on a balance. It would require frequent writing of factors of 10^{-24} if we expressed masses of atoms in grams. It is convenient to choose the mass of the lightest known atom, that of a hydrogen atom, as the *unified atomic mass unit* (u). Table 9.1 lists the atomic masses of some common elements in both grams and unified atomic mass units.*

Table 9.1

Atom	Mass (g)	(u)	atom	Mass (g)	(u)
Aluminum	4.48×10^{-23}	27.0	Mercury	3.34×10^{-22}	201
Calcium	6.66×10^{-23}	40.1	Nickel	9.75×10^{-23}	58.7
Carbon	1.99×10^{-23}	12.0	Nitrogen	2.33×10^{-23}	14.0
Chlorine	5.89×10^{-23}	35.5	Oxygen	2.66×10^{-23}	16.0
Copper	1.05×10^{-22}	63.5	Phosphorus	5.15×10^{-23}	31.0
Gold	3.27×10^{-22}	197	Potassium	6.49×10^{-23}	39.1
Helium	6.64×10^{-24}	4.00	Sodium	3.82×10^{-23}	23.0
Hydrogen	1.66×10^{-24}	1.01	Strontium	1.45×10^{-22}	87.6
Iodine	2.11×10^{-22}	127	Sulfur	5.33×10^{-23}	32.1
Iron	9.27×10^{-23}	55.8	Thorium	3.85×10^{-22}	232
Lead	3.44×10^{-22}	207	Tin	1.98×10^{-23}	119
Lithium	1.15×10^{-23}	6.94	Uranium	3.95×10^{-22}	238
Magnesium	4.04×10^{-23}	24.3	Zinc	1.09×10^{-22}	65.4

*Today a unified atomic mass unit is defined differently, but the mass of a hydrogen atom, using the modern definition, is very close to 1 u. The masses given in Table 9.1 are based on the modern definition of a unified atomic mass unit.

16. How many atoms of aluminum are there in 1.0×10^{-3} g of aluminum?

17. a. If 90% of a sample of polonium remains after 21 days, what percent of the original sample remains after 42 days? 63 days? 84 days? 105 days? 126 days?

b. Plot a graph of the percent of atoms remaining as a function of time in days. How does your graph compare with the graph in Figure 9.9?

18. Using Table 9.1, calculate the mass of a polonium atom in unified mass units.

19. Suppose that the smallest mass that you can measure on your balance is 0.005 g. What is the smallest number of carbon atoms that you could mass on your balance?

20. Write a brief summary of the steps followed in finding the mass of polonium atoms by radioactive decay.

9.6 Atomic Masses and Molecular Formulas

Now that we know the masses of single atoms of the elements, we can find out how many atoms of one element there are for each atom of the other element in a compound made of two elements. Once we know this, we can write down the simplest formula for the compound. To see how this is possible, we shall consider the example of a liquid compound of carbon and chlorine. In this compound the ratio of the mass of chlorine to the mass of carbon has been found by experiment to be 11.8.

Let us assume that the compound contains equal numbers of carbon and chlorine atoms. Then, since the mass of a chlorine atom is 35.5 u and that of a carbon atom is 12.0 u (see Table 9.1), the chlorine atoms would have a mass of

$$\frac{35.5 \text{ u}}{12.0 \text{ u}} = 2.96$$

times that of carbon atoms. Therefore, we should expect the mass of chlorine in the compound to be 2.96 times the mass of carbon. But we know that there is 11.8 times as much chlorine as carbon in the compound. Our assumption that the compound contains equal numbers of carbon and chlorine atoms was wrong.

The observed mass ratio is 11.8/2.96 = 4 times larger than the one predicted on the assumption of equal numbers of carbon and chlorine atoms in the compound. Now we can see what the answer is: There must be four times as many chlorine atoms as there are carbon atoms in the compound.

Indeed

$$\frac{4 \times 35.5 \text{ u}}{12.0 \text{ u}} = 11.8,$$

the observed mass ratio. The simplest formula for the compound is, therefore, CCl_4. Its name is "carbon tetrachloride."

Carbon tetrachloride boils at 77°C. The resulting gas is made up of molecules containing one atom of carbon for every four atoms of chlorine. But on the basis of our calculation alone, we cannot tell how many atoms of carbon and chlorine actually cluster together to form a molecule; the simplest formula is CCl_4, but C_2Cl_8 or C_3Cl_{12}, for example, cannot be ruled out as the correct molecular formula.

Liquids and solids may not be made up of molecules at all. For these cases, we are free to choose the simplest formula to describe the composition of the compound. By extension of the reasoning we have used to determine the simplest formula of carbon tetrachloride, we can write the simplest formulas for compounds containing more than two elements.

21. What is the ratio of the mass of carbon to the mass of oxygen in carbon dioxide (CO_2)?

22. Use Table 9.1 to find the mass, in unified atomic mass units, of a molecule of phosphorus pentachloride (PCl_5).

23. In Section 6.2 you found that the mass ratio of hydrogen to oxygen in water is 0.13. Using Table 9.1, write the simplest formula for water.

24. The ratio for the mass of chlorine to iron in iron dichloride is 127/100. Use the information from Table 9.1 to determine the simplest formula for iron dichloride.

▶ For Review, Applications, and Extensions

25. A rectangular object 3.0 cm × 4.0 cm × 5.0 cm is made of many tiny cubes, each 1.0×10^{-2} cm on an edge. How many cubes does the object contain?

26. The diameter of a tennis ball is about 0.07 m, and the dimensions of a tennis court are about 10 m × 24 m. How many tennis balls will be required to cover the court?

27. Spherical lead shot are poured into a square tray, 10 cm on a side, until they completely cover the bottom. The shot are poured from the tray into a graduated cylinder, which they fill to the 20-cm³ mark.
    a. What is the diameter of a single shot?
    b. How many shot were in the tray?
    c. If the 20 cm³ of shot had a mass of 130 g, what would be the mass of a single shot?

28. If the molecules of the oleic acid layer you made could be placed end to end in a line, about how long would it be?

29. If a 10^{-3}-g sample of radium produces 4×10^7 counts/min, how much radium would give 100 counts/min?

30. The rate of decay of the sample of polonium described in this chapter had a counting rate of 4.4×10^{13} counts/min. How does this number compare with the number of seconds in a million years?

31. Suppose you buy a 2-kg bag of dried beans that has been contaminated with small stones. How would you go about finding the approximate number of stones in the bag without separating all the stones in the bag from the beans? What assumptions have you made?

32. A cubic millimeter (10^{-3} cm^3) of blood is found to contain about 5×10^6 red blood cells. The volume of blood in an adult human body is about 5×10^3 cm^3. About how many red blood cells are there in an adult human body?

33. Some polonium is dissolved in 1,000 cm^3 of nitric acid, and a 0.01-cm^3 sample of the solution is counted. Then the number of disintegrations per minute is found to be 3×10^3. How many disintegrations per minute occurred in the original solution?

34. If 10^{18} atoms of polonium disintegrate to produce lead and 10^{-5} g of helium, what is the mass of a helium atom?

35. a. What size fraction of a sample of pure polonium will decay in 100 days? (See Figure 9.9.)
    b. If a counter initially records 5×10^4 counts/min for the sample, what should you expect it to record after 100 days?

36. Using the atomic masses of zinc and chlorine in Table 9.1, return to the data you obtained from Experiment 6.4, The Synthesis of Zinc Chloride, and determine the simplest formula for zinc chloride.

37. Compared to gases, solids are practically incompressible. The atomic model can account for this by considering atoms to be hard spheres that touch one another. Applying this idea provides a way to calculate the diameter of one atom of polonium.

    a. Use the mass of polonium that decayed (Section 9.5) and the density of polonium (9.4 g/cm^3) to find the volume of polonium that decayed.

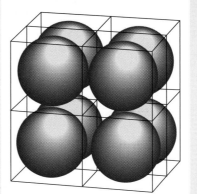

Figure A

For Problem 37

Spheres touching all the faces of the cubes containing them. The diameter of the spheres equals the length of the edge of the cubes.

b. Using your answer to part (a) and the number of atoms of polonium that decayed, find the volume of one atom of polonium.

c. Assume that the atoms of polonium are arranged as shown in Figure A. What is the diameter of one atom of polonium?

d. Why is it important that we assume that in a solid, atoms touch one another?

38. In Question 37 you first divided the mass of the sample by the density of the solid to find the volume of the sample. You then divided the volume of the sample by the number of atoms in the sample to find the volume of one atom. You may also do these two operations in the opposite order.

a. What is the result of first dividing the mass of the sample by the number of atoms in the sample?

b. What remains to be done to find the volume of one atom?

c. Using data from Table 9.1 and Table 3.1 (page 52), calculate the volume of one atom of each of these elements: aluminum, iron, and gold.

39. What value do you find for the volume of one atom of helium when you calculate it from the experimental data in the chapter and the equation below?

$$\text{Volume of one atom} = \frac{\text{volume of gas sample}}{\text{number of atoms in gas sample}}$$

THEMES FOR SHORT ESSAYS

1. A few grains of sand can be placed on an overhead projector and projected on the wall. The images are large enough to be measured with a ruler. To be able to calculate the size of the grains of sand, you also need to project an object of known size. Do this investigation and find the size of one sand grain. Then, using the results of your own experimentation on the volume of sand (Experiment 1.4, Measuring Volume by Displacement of Water), write a research report, "The Number of Sand Grains in a Cup of Sand."

2. Write an experimental section for an *IBS* (*Introductory Biological Science*) textbook to count the hairs on a human head.

10

The Classification of Elements: The Periodic Table

Al	Si	P
27.0	28.1	31.0

Zn	Ga	Ge	As
65.4	69.7	72.6	74.9

Cd	In	Sn	Sb
112.4	114.8	118.7	121.8

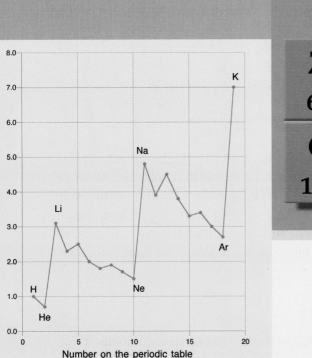

10.1 Introduction

By now you have accumulated a fair amount of knowledge about elements and their atoms. Elements have characteristic properties that distinguish them from one another. These properties do not depend on the size of the sample on which they are measured (Chapter 3). However, the sample must be large enough so that the mass, volume, and temperature can be measured to determine density, melting point, and boiling point.

You have seen that single atoms of each element have properties that are different from the properties of a sample of measurable size. For example, they have a mass (Section 9.5). Atoms of different elements have different spectra (Sections 8.6–8.8). Atoms that form compounds do so in specific ratios (Sections 8.4 and 9.6). These ratios are related to the ratios that express the law of constant proportions (Section 6.5).

To find any kind of regularity among the properties of elements and their atoms, we must choose a property by which to order the elements. We will choose atomic mass, as was done historically.

Suppose we list the elements in order of increasing atomic mass. Will elements with similar properties be listed next to one another? For example, are the masses of atoms that combine in a one-to-one ratio with chlorine generally lighter than elements that combine in a different ratio? Do all elements that are made up of such atoms have other properties in common, that is, are they "similar" to one another? To answer these questions, we shall first explore in some detail what we mean by "similar" elements.

10.2 Classifying Elements

Deciding whether or not two elements are similar involves subjective judgment. We will illustrate this with the elements listed in Table 10.1. All these elements occur in nature as free elements. (This does not mean that none of them are ever found in compounds.)

Being found as free elements is the only property common to all the elements in the table. As a next step, we may separate the gases from the

Table 10.1		
Argon (Ar)	Krypton (Kr)	Oxygen (O)
Carbon (C)	Mercury (Hg)	Palladium (Pd)
Copper (Cu)	Neon (Ne)	Platinum (Pt)
Gold (Au)	Nitrogen (N)	Silver (Ag)
Helium (He)	Osmium (Os)	Sulfur (S)

solids. Are there properties shared by all the gases in the table, or is there some criterion that would suggest a further subdivision?

Argon, helium, krypton, and neon do not combine with any other elements to form compounds. They are *noble gases.** In fact, the noble gases are monatomic: their atoms will not even join together to form diatomic molecules of the element (Section 8.5). It seems reasonable to call them similar and put them in a group by themselves.

Nitrogen and oxygen, on the other hand, are diatomic and also form compounds with other elements. They make up 99% of the atmosphere. But is it useful to put nitrogen and oxygen in a group by themselves? Does either or both of them have properties in common with other elements not found free in nature? If so, it would be more useful to classify them in different groups. This is again a matter of judgment.

Two other elements, the metals aluminum (Al) and iron (Fe), do not occur in nature as free elements. They have quite different properties from each other. However, some of their compounds have similar properties. In particular, some of their compounds are soluble in water. When these solutions are electrolyzed, the elements collect at the negative electrode. (This process is called *plating*.) Are these similarities enough to put aluminum and iron in the same group of elements?

1. **Leaving out the six gases in Table 10.1, try to divide the remaining nine elements into metals and nonmetals. To do this, first identify the elements with which you are familiar. Which are metals and which are not?**

10.3 The Extraction of Similar Elements from Similar Compounds

Compounds with similar properties are likely to contain elements with similar properties. Furthermore, if two compounds have similar properties, we would expect to be able to separate their elements by using similar methods. Consider, for example, the two compounds in Table 10.2

Table 10.2			
Substance	Color	Density (g/cm³)	Melting point (°C)
Caustic potash	white	2.0	360
Caustic soda	white	2.1	318

*Not until 70 years after their discovery were compounds of Kr and two other noble gases (not listed in Table 10.1) synthesized. Most are not stable at room temperat

Both substances are very corrosive, are very soluble in water, and their water solutions have a soapy feel. Furthermore, both solids readily absorb moisture from the air to form a solution. We can electrolyze both solutions: However, no metal plates out at the negative electrode. Instead, hydrogen is released. This is what happened in Experiment 6.2, The Decomposition of Water, when you used sodium carbonate.

In 1807 Sir Humphry Davy discovered and isolated the metallic element potassium from caustic potash. He melted the caustic potash by heating it above 360°C and then electrolyzed the liquid compound. Next, he produced the metallic element sodium by applying the same method to caustic soda.

Not surprisingly, perhaps, the properties of these two metallic elements, sodium and potassium, are very similar. Both are shiny and silvery in color, soft, and malleable. Both combine with oxygen at room temperature, unlike copper, for example, which must be strongly heated. Both react violently with water at room temperature. (So much heat is generated so rapidly, in fact, that the hydrogen produced often ignites spontaneously.) Both elements are good conductors of heat and electric charge. Both have densities, melting points, and boiling points that are much lower than those of most common metals.

2. **Why was it necessary for Humphry Davy to use molten caustic potash and caustic soda rather than their water solutions to produce potassium and sodium?**

3. **Why are deposits of pure sodium metal or pure potassium metal not seen in nature?**

Alkali Metals, Alkaline Earth Metals, ... gens

...w more elements were separated from their compounds. ...oups of elements with similar properties could be

19...

...ents listed in Table 10.3, which were produced by ... used to produce potassium and sodium (Sec-

... can also subdivide this group of similar ele- ...ups. One group contains lithium, potassium, and ... same ratio of atoms in their oxides (2:1) and in ... This group is called the *alkali metals*. The other ...gnesium, and strontium—also have the same ratio

Table 10.3

Element	Compound	
	Oxide	Chloride
Calcium	CaO	$CaCl_2$
Lithium	Li_2O	LiCl
Magnesium	MgO	$MgCl_2$
Potassium	K_2O	KCl
Sodium	Na_2O	NaCl
Strontium	SrO	$SrCl_2$

for their oxides (1:1) and for their chlorides (1:2). This group is called the *alkaline earth metals*. Alkaline earth metals resemble the alkali metals and are found in common rocks in various compounds.

Table 10.4 contains a group of elements that form similar compounds with sodium, calcium, and hydrogen. We could have expanded the table by including many more compounds. Even if we had done so, the similarities would still hold true.

Table 10.4

Element	Sodium compound	Calcium compound	Hydrogen compound
Bromine	NaBr	$CaBr_2$	HBr
Chlorine	NaCl	$CaCl_2$	HCl
Fluorine	NaF	CaF_2	HF
Iodine	NaI	CaI_2	HI

All four elements in the table are very closely related by their properties. They are all highly reactive and thus are not found as free elements in nature. The sodium compounds of these elements, listed in the table, are also very similar. They all form colorless crystals, they are all soluble in water, and they do not decompose easily. The elements in this group are called *halogens*.

In an electrolysis of their sodium compounds, these elements will move to the positive electrode, just as did the oxygen in Experiment 6.2, The Decomposition of Water. Whether they can be collected depends on the material from which the electrode is made. For example, if you had used an iron electrode rather than one made from stainless steel when you electrolyzed water, much of the oxygen would have combined with the iron to form rust.

4. **Break up Table 10.3 into two tables, one with only alkali metals and one with only alkaline earth metals.**

5. **How can you use the combining ratios to distinguish the alkali metals from the alkaline earth metals?**

6. **Examine Tables 10.3 and 10.4.**
   a. **What is the combining ratio of potassium with bromine, fluorine, and iodine?**
   b. **Write the formulas for the potassium compounds referred to in part (a).**

ACTIVITY

10.5 Atomic Mass and Other Properties of Atoms

In the discussion so far, we have intentionally selected elements that can be easily classified according to their properties: noble gases, alkali metals, alkaline earth metals, and halogens. We now ask, Are the masses of atoms of the elements in each of these groups close to one another?

To answer this question, we have summarized some important properties of 24 elements and recorded them individually on 24 cards for ease of comparison (Figure 10.1). Each element is identified by its name, its symbol, the mass of a single atom (u) of the element, and its common combining ratio with chlorine. For elements that can be produced by electrolysis, we list the electrode to which they move during the process.

Figure 10.1

A sample element card.

To begin, arrange all the element cards in a single horizontal row in order of increasing mass from left to right. When you have done this correctly, hydrogen (H) will appear at the far left and krypton (Kr) will be at the far right. Identify the noble gases. To highlight their location, move each card of a noble gas slightly toward you.

• Are the noble gases near one another in the sequence?

Let us now check the location of elements belonging to the halogens. Identify these elements and move their cards slightly toward you, as you did with the noble gases.

- Are the elements of the halogen group near one another in this ordering?

Notice that the halogens are near the noble gases. All occur immediately to the left of a noble gas, with the exception of chlorine. Chlorine is separated from argon by potassium. To place chlorine immediately to the left of argon, we must disrupt the ascending order of the atomic masses. This can be done in two ways. Either interchange chlorine and potassium or interchange potassium and argon. To help you judge which interchange will cause less disruption, copy Figure 10.2 into your notebook and graph the atomic masses for both sequences. (You may want to use Os for the upper sequence and Xs for the lower one.)

- To place chlorine immediately to the left of argon, which elements should you interchange? Do it!

To see the usefulness of this interchange, arrange the elements from hydrogen to argon in the following way:

(1) Arrange the noble gases to form a column, so that each noble gas represents the right-most element in a row, as shown in Figure 10.3.

(2) Place the other elements in the rows to the left of the noble gases. Be sure to keep the elements in order of increasing atomic mass from left to right within each row, as in Figure 10.3.

(3) Put the remaining cards (potassium through krypton) aside for future use.

- Does each of the noble gases have the highest atomic mass in its row? If not, recheck the ordering of your elements.

- Ignoring hydrogen for the moment, to what group do the elements in the first column on the left belong? the second column? the seventh column?

- Consider the properties of hydrogen. In which column, if any, do you think it belongs? Why?

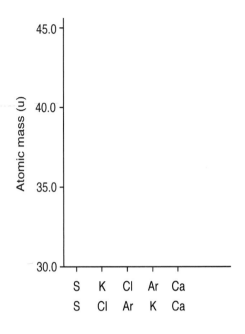

Figure 10.2

The axes for a graph of the atomic masses for the elements from sulfur to calcium. In the upper sequence, chlorine and potassium have been interchanged, and in the lower sequence, potassium and argon have been interchanged.

Figure 10.3

The proposed arrangement of the elements from hydrogen to argon in three rows. The noble gases appear in the right-most column.

10.6 The Elements in the Third Through Sixth Columns

Before you started ordering elements by their atomic masses, you already knew something about some groups of elements. Specifically, the noble gases, the halogens, the alkali metals, and the alkaline earth metals displayed similar properties within each group. Thus, when you started rearranging elements to construct a table in the preceding activity, it was reassuring to see that each of the first, second, seventh, and eighth columns contained elements of only one group.

What about the elements in the third through the sixth columns? Do the elements in each of these columns have similar properties? Do the properties of elements in any column differ from the properties of the elements in the adjacent columns?

Comparing the properties of boron and aluminum shows that they have much less in common than, for example, lithium and sodium. (See Sections 10.3 and 10.4.) Boron is a black powder and a nonmetal. Like other nonmetals, it is a poor conductor of heat and cannot be produced by electrolysis. Aluminum is a shiny metal that can be produced by electrolysis; it is collected at the negative electrode. Yet boron and aluminum generally combine in the same atomic ratios with other elements. For example, in addition to the chlorides BCl_3 and $AlCl_3$ listed on the cards, they form similar oxides, B_2O_3 and Al_2O_3. Thus, as we said earlier, placing elements in groups is a matter of judgment. Whether the judgment is good or bad is determined by the usefulness of the grouping.

The situation is somewhat simpler when we compare the properties of carbon and silicon in the fourth column. Neither of these elements is a metal and neither can be produced by electrolysis. Both form many compounds with other elements in the same atomic ratios. For example, in addition to CCl_4 and $SiCl_4$ listed on the cards, they form CH_4 and SiH_4, and CO_2 and SiO_2.

The sixth column has some problems. Although both oxygen and sulfur combine in the same ratio with hydrogen (H_2O and H_2S), many other compounds are dissimilar. However, keeping sulfur in the sixth column leaves other elements of known groups in their respective columns. Later in the chapter we shall develop better arguments in favor of the placement of sulfur.

10. **Boron and aluminum are both in the third column of your table. Which of the following properties do they share?**
    A. Color
    B. Classification as a metal
    C. Produced by electrolysis
    D. Combining ratio with chlorine
    E. Combining ratio with oxygen

A C T I V I T Y

10.7 The Elements in the Fourth Row

Reconstruct the table of elements the way you left it at the end of Section 10.5. Form a fourth row with the remaining cards, with krypton in the column with the noble gases. (We intentionally did not provide enough elements to complete the row.)

• Which of the elements can you confidently place in their proper columns?

• What are the difficulties in placing the remaining elements?

10.8 The Fourth and Fifth Rows: A Historical Perspective

The preceding activity ended with a difficulty: How can we fit copper, zinc, and other elements into a table so that elements with similar properties will appear in vertical columns. In addition, the atomic mass should increase in each row, at least in most cases.

The Russian chemist Dmitri Mendeleev (pronounced MEN-duh-LAY-uff) first proposed such a table in 1871. The first five rows of a modern version of his table are shown in Figure 10.4 on the next page. Because the elements are arranged in a pattern that repeats, the table is called the *periodic table* of the elements. The rows in the table are often referred to as *periods*. A complete periodic table of the elements may be on display in your science classroom.

H 1.0																	He 4.0
Li 6.9	Be 9.0											B 10.8	C 12.0	N 14.0	O 16.0	F 19.0	Ne 20.2
Na 23.0	Mg 24.3											Al 27.0	Si 28.1	P 31.0	S 32.1	Cl 35.5	Ar 39.9
K 39.1	Ca 40.1	Sc 45.0	Ti 47.9	V 50.9	Cr 52.0	Mn 54.9	Fe 55.8	Co 58.9	Ni 58.7	Cu 63.5	Zn 65.4	Ga 69.7	Ge 72.6	As 74.9	Se 79.0	Br 79.9	Kr 83.8
Rb 85.5	Sr 87.6	Y 88.9	Zr 91.2	Nb 92.9	Mo 95.9	Te 98.9	Ru 101.1	Rh 102.9	Pd 106.4	Ag 107.9	Cd 112.4	In 114.8	Sn 118.7	Sb 121.8	Te 127.6	I 126.9	Xe 131.3

Figure 10.4

The first five rows of the periodic table. The shaded elements had not yet been discovered when Mendeleev proposed his table.

We can look at the periodic table as a model. To be useful a model must accomplish two goals: (1) it must account for and organize known facts. (2) The model must enable us to make testable predictions (Section 8.1). Was this table useful when it was proposed?

Let us examine Figure 10.4 more closely. Except for hydrogen, all elements in the first column are alkali metals. All elements in the second column are alkaline earth metals. By inserting new columns in the fourth and fifth row, Mendeleev succeeded in keeping the remaining groups in vertical columns. The elements in the column headed by carbon all form similar compounds with other elements.

Although it is still difficult to see why oxygen and sulfur are in the same column, the elements below sulfur have much in common with sulfur. For example, their oxides—SO_2, SeO_2, TeO_2—all dissolve in water and form similar acids. All (including oxygen) combine with hydrogen in the same ratio: H_2O, H_2S, H_2Se, and H_2Te. The periodic table clearly accounts for and organizes these and other facts known about the elements.

The amazing achievement of Mendeleev is the use of the periodic table to make predictions. The elements shaded in yellow and blue in Table 10.4 were not yet discovered when he proposed the table. For the ones shaded yellow, he left empty spaces and gave them temporary names. Moreover, on the basis of the properties of adjacent elements, he predicted what their properties would be. Within fifteen years all three elements were discovered. Their properties were indeed close to what Mendeleev predicted.

Particularly impressive was his prediction about the properties of the element that he called "eka-silicon" ("following silicon"). It is called *germanium* (Ge) today. A comparison between the predicted properties and the observed properties is shown in Table 10.5.

Table 10.5

Property	Eka-silicon	Germanium
Atomic mass (u)	72	72.6
Density (g/cm³)	5.5	5.47
Color	dirty gray	grayish white
Density of oxide (g/cm³)	4.7	4.70
Density of chloride (g/cm³)	1.9	1.89
Boiling point of chloride (°C)	< 100	86

Today, with much more experimental and theoretical knowledge, we understand the periodic table in a deeper way. But, as usual in science, such an understanding brings with it new questions and new challenges.

11. Cesium (Cs) appears on the complete periodic table in the first column. What do you expect its properties to be?

12. The element barium appears on the complete periodic table in the second column. What do you expect the molecular formula to be for the compound formed from barium and oxygen? from barium and chlorine?

For Review, Applications, and Extensions

13. Radon (see Section 7.7) is a noble gas.
    a. How does this fact explain why radon can reach the surface of the earth?
    b. Why does radon accumulate in basements rather than in higher floors?

14. Why do you think America's Declaration of Independence is stored in a sealed case containing only helium?

15. Silver, gold, and platinum are used in jewelry. What properties do they have in common for this use?

16. Mercury is a liquid at room temperature and is considered to be a metal. Why is this so?

17. A student claims that oxygen and sulfur should not be in the same group because one is a gas and the other is a solid at room temperature. What can you say to counter this claim?

18. a. Examine Figure 10.4. Aside from potassium and argon, are there other exceptions to the ascending order of atomic mass?

    b. How does the mass difference between the interchanged elements compare with the difference in atomic mass between potassium and argon?

    c. For one of the pairs of elements that you identified in part (a), give a reason why the interchange was made.

Theme for a Short Essay

Before publishing his periodic table, Dmitri Mendeleev presented his ideas in a lecture to the Russian Chemical Society. Suppose you had attended that lecture as a science reporter for a newspaper. Write a brief report of the lecture.

Appendix: Calculating in Scientific Notation

Part 1 Scientific Notation

The number of atoms in a piece of iron is very large. The mass of one atom in grams is a very small number. Scientific notation simplifies calculations made with large and small numbers by eliminating the need to use zeros as placeholders. Scientific notation thus enables us to write only the significant digits of a number.

The numbers in shorthand in Table A.1 are called *powers of ten*. The small numeral at the right of 10 is called the *exponent*. It is evident that the exponent of 10 equals the number of zeros in the standard notation. Numbers larger than 1 have trailing zeros and numbers smaller than 1 have leading zeros. In order to distinguish between the two types of numbers, we write a minus sign before the exponent for numbers smaller than 1.

Table A.1

Words	Standard numerals	Written shorthand	Spoken shorthand
million	1,000,000	10^6	"ten to the sixth"
hundred thousand	100,000	10^5	"ten to the fifth"
ten thousand	10,000	10^4	"ten to the fourth"
thousand	1,000	10^3	"ten cubed"
hundred	100	10^2	"ten squared"
ten	10	(10^1)	(shorthand not used)
one	1	(10^0)	(shorthand not used)
tenth	0.1	10^{-1}	"ten to the negative one"
hundredth	0.01	10^{-2}	"ten to the negative two"
thousandth	0.001	10^{-3}	"ten to the negative three"

Any number can be written as a product of a number between 1 and 10, and a power of ten. The following examples show how this is done.

$$3{,}000 = 3 \times 1{,}000 = 3 \times 10^3$$

$$3{,}200 = 3.2 \times 1{,}000 = 3.2 \times 10^3$$

$$0.05 = 5 \times 0.01 = 5 \times 10^{-2}$$

$$0.058 = 5.8 \times 0.01 = 5.8 \times 10^{-2}$$

The number multiplying a power of ten is called the *coefficient*. A number that is written as a product of a coefficient between 1 and 10 and a power of ten is said to be written in *scientific notation*.

You can think of the process of separating a number into a coefficient and a power of ten in the following way. Moving a decimal point three places to the left divides a number by 1,000; for example,

$$3,200 \div 1,000 = 3.2.$$

To keep the value of the number unchanged, you have to multiply it by 1,000. Hence $3,200 = 3.2 \times 1,000$. (In 3,200 the decimal point after the last zero is not written.)

Moving a decimal point two places to the right multiplies a number by 100. To keep the number 0.058 unchanged after moving the decimal point two places to the right, you must divide the new form—5.8—by 100, or multiply it by 0.01. Hence $0.058 = 5.8 \times 10^{-2}$.

1. **Write the following numbers as numerals with exponents.**
   a. hundred million   b. billion   c. ten thousand
   d. millionth   e. ten millionth   f. billionth

   (*Hint:* **For numbers smaller than one, always include the zero to the left of the decimal point; for example, 0.01,** *not* **.01.**)

2. **Write the following numbers as standard numerals and in words.**

   a. 10^7 b. 10^{10} c. 10^{-5} d. 10^{-7}

3. **Write the following numbers in scientific notation.**
   a. 8,000,000   b. 400,000   c. 370,000
   d. 5,610   e. 423   f. 9,060

4. **Write the following numbers in scientific notation.**
   a. 0.6   b. 0.07   c. 0.004
   d. 0.0506   e. 0.00042   f. 0.612

5. **Write the following numbers as standard numerals.**
   a. 3×10^6 b. 4.02×10^8 c. 6.52×10^7
   d. 8×10^{-5} e. 7.2×10^{-3} f. 4.07×10^{-4}

Part 2 Multiplying and Dividing in Scientific Notation: Significant Digits

As a preparation for multiplying numbers in scientific notation, let us look first at products of powers of ten:

$$10^3 \times 10^2 = 1,000 \times 100 = 100,000 = 10^5$$
$$10^6 \times 10^{-4} = 1,000,000 \times 0.0001 = 100 = 10^2$$
$$10^1 \times 10^{-1} = 10 \times 0.1 = 1 = 10^{-5}$$
$$10^{-2} \times 10^{-5} = 0.01 \times 0.00001 = 0.0000001 = 10^{-7}$$

You can work out other examples, which will lead to the general rule: To multiply powers, add the exponents (with their proper signs!). Thus, in the preceding examples, we could have found the exponents of the products by addition:

$$3 + 2 = 5$$
$$6 + (-4) = 2$$
$$1 + (-1) = 0$$
$$(-2) + (-5) = -7$$

To multiply numbers in scientific notation, change the order of the factors in a product. For example:

$$(3 \times 10^5) \times (2 \times 10^4) = (3 \times 2) \times (10^5 \times 10^4) = 6 \times 10^9$$
$$(1.5 \times 10^{-2}) \times (3.0 \times 10^6) = (1.5 \times 3.0) \times (10^{-2} \times 10^6) = 4.5 \times 10^4$$

In general, to multiply two or more numbers in scientific notation, multiply the coefficients and the powers of ten separately.

Since powers of ten are multiplied by adding their exponents, it is reasonable to expect that powers of ten are divided by subtracting their exponents. The following examples illustrate this rule.

$$\frac{10^7}{10^4} = \frac{10,000,000}{10,000} = 1,000 = 10^3 \qquad\qquad 7 - 4 = 3$$

$$\frac{10^{-2}}{10^3} = \frac{0.01}{1,000} = 0.00001 = 10^{-5} \qquad\qquad (-2) - 3 = -5$$

$$\frac{10^2}{10^{-2}} = \frac{100}{0.01} = 10,000 = 10^4 \qquad\qquad 2 - (-2) = 4$$

$$\frac{10^{-3}}{10^{-2}} = \frac{0.001}{0.01} = 0.1 = 10^{-1} \qquad\qquad (-3) - (-2) = -1$$

To divide numbers in scientific notation, rearrange the numbers in a way similar to that used in multiplication.

$$\frac{6 \times 10^7}{2 \times 10^5} = \frac{6}{2} \times \frac{10^7}{10^5} = 3 \times 10^2$$

$$\frac{4.5 \times 10^{-2}}{1.5 \times 10^{-4}} = \frac{4.5}{1.5} \times \frac{10^{-2}}{10^{-4}} = 3.0 \times 10^2$$

In general, to divide numbers in scientific notation, divide the coefficients and the powers of ten separately.

Note that when two numbers in scientific notation are multiplied or divided, the product or quotient is not automatically given in scientific notation. For example,

$$5 \times 10^2 \times 7 \times 10^4 = 35 \times 10^6$$

Here the coefficient, 35, is not between 1 and 10. However, we can move the decimal point one place to the left, and compensate for this by multiplying the number by 10:

$$35 \times 10^6 = 3.5 \times 10 \times 10^6 = 3.5 \times 10^7$$

Here is another example:

$$\frac{4 \times 10^5}{8 \times 10^2} = 0.5 \times 10^3$$

To change the coefficient to a number between 1 and 10, in this case you move the decimal point one place to the right, and compensate for this by dividing by 10 (or multiplying by 10^{-1}):

$$0.5 \times 10^3 = 5 \times 10^{-1} \times 10^3 = 5 \times 10^2$$

Scientific notation eliminates the need for zeros as placeholders. It removes any doubt about the significance of zeros in a measured number. For example, how many significant digits are there in 3,600 cm^2? Is this accurate to the nearest 100 cm^2, 10 cm^2, or 1 cm^2? If standard numerals are used, there is no way of telling. In scientific notation, however, you write 3.6×10^3 cm^2 to indicate two significant digits, and 3.60×10^3 cm^2 to indicate three significant digits. Thus, you would write 3.60×10^3 cm^2 if the measurement 3,600 cm^2 were reliable to the nearest 10 cm^2.

You are likely to use scientific notation mostly for calculations with measurements. You should therefore use the rule given in Section 3.4 for the number of digits to be written when multiplying or dividing the coefficients: The result should have as many digits as the measurement with the smallest number of digits.

6. Multiply the following numbers.

   a. $10^8 \times 10^6$ b. $10^9 \times 10^{-5}$ c. $10^{-2} \times 10^6$

   d. $10^{-3} \times 10^{-3}$ e. $10^4 \times 10^{-7}$ f. $10^{-10} \times 10^{-12}$

7. Multiply the following numbers and express the results in scientific notation.

   a. $2 \times 10^7 \times 3 \times 10^{-4}$ b. $4 \times 10^3 \times 4 \times 10^3$

   c. $5 \times 10^{-2} \times 1 \times 10^{-6}$ d. $7 \times 10^3 \times 5 \times 10^{-2}$

   e. $2.5 \times 10^4 \times 3 \times 10^5$ f. $6 \times 10^7 \times 1.5 \times 10^8$

8. Divide the following numbers.

   a. $\dfrac{10^7}{10^3}$ b. $\dfrac{10^4}{10^8}$ c. $\dfrac{10^{12}}{10^{-2}}$

   d. $\dfrac{10^{-6}}{10^{-8}}$ e. $\dfrac{10^{-4}}{10^3}$ f. $\dfrac{10^{-4}}{10^{-2}}$

9. Divide the following numbers and express the results in scientific notation.

   a. $\dfrac{6 \times 10^5}{4 \times 10^3}$ b. $\dfrac{2 \times 10^7}{5 \times 10^{-8}}$ c. $\dfrac{7 \times 10^{-4}}{1 \times 10^{-6}}$

   d. $\dfrac{2 \times 10^8}{8 \times 10^4}$ e. $\dfrac{3 \times 10^{-2}}{6 \times 10^4}$ f. $\dfrac{7 \times 10^5}{2 \times 10^2}$

10. Write the following measurements in scientific notation.

    a. 6,500 g to the nearest 100 g

    b. 6,500 g to the nearest 1 g

    c. 6,500 g to the nearest 0.1 g

    d. 200 cm^3 to the nearest 1 cm^3

    e. 5,040 cm^3 to the nearest 10 cm^3

    f. 70,000 cm^3 to the nearest 1,000 cm^3

11. What is the area of a rectangular piece of land with each pair of sides?

    a. 3.5×10^3 m and 1.2×10^3 m

    b. 6.3×10^2 m and 4.7×10^4 m

12. Calculate the mass of 2.0×10^4 cm^3 of oxygen. (See Table 3.1 on page 52 for the density of oxygen.)

13. Suppose that a 3.2×10^{-3} g sample of a radioactive element produces 4.5×10^4 helium atoms per minute. How many helium atoms would be produced by 1.00 g of the element in 60.0 minutes?

Epilogue

As this course comes to an end, you may ask yourself: "What have I learned this year in science?" We hope that you will think of several things, some specific and some general.

During the year we tried to familiarize you with some of the basic facts and ideas of physical science. You saw the evidence for the facts, and the usefulness of the ideas. Contrary to what you may have expected, science does not deal with absolute truths. The specific facts we find in the laboratory, such as density, melting points, solubilities, and half-lives, are all subject to the limitations of our measurements.

Scientific laws are generalizations based on measurements made many times under controlled conditions to assure their validity. Yet these generalizations also have their limitations. If this is the case in science, how careful must you be about the facts and generalizations in your daily life? Do you ask for evidence to support what you read and hear? If this introduction to science has made you a more critical reader, a more careful observer, and a sharper thinker, your work during the year was worthwhile.

Acknowledgments from the First Edition

The following members of the Educational Services Incorporated staff in addition to myself were involved in the development of the course; John B. Coulter, on leave from Pakuranga College, Howick, New Zealand; Judson B. Cross; John H. Dodge; Robert W. Estin, on leave from Roosevelt University, Chicago, Illinois; Malcolm H. Forbes; Ervin H. Hoffart; Gerardo Melcher, on leave from the University of Chile, Santiago, Chile; Harold A. Pratt, on leave from Jefferson County Public Schools, Lakewood, Colorado; Louis E. Smith, on leave from San Diego State College, San Diego, California; Darrel W. Tomer, on leave from Hanford Union High School, Hanford, California; and James A. Walter.

For the summer of 1963, we were joined by Elmer L. Galley, Mott Program of the Flint Public Schools, Flint, Michigan; Edward A. Shore, The Putney School, Putney, Vermont; and Byron L. Youtz, Reed College, Portland, Oregon.

Later on, considerable time was devoted to this project by others who joined us during the summers or consulted on a part-time basis throughout the following years; Gilbert H. Daenzer, Lutheran High School Central, St. Louis, Missouri; Thomas J. Dillon, Concord- Carlisle High School, Concord, Massachusetts; Winslow Durgin, Xavier High School, Concord, Massachusetts; Alan Holden, Bell Telephone Laboratories, Murray Hill, New Jersey; Robert Gardner, Salisbury School, Salisbury, Connecticut; Father John Kerdiejus, S.J. Xavier High School, Concord, Massachusetts; Herman H. Kirkpatrick, Roosevelt High School, Des Moines, Iowa; Elisabeth Lincoln, Dana Hall School, Wellesley, Massachusetts; John V. Manuelian, Warren Junior High School, Newton, Massachusetts; John N. Meade, Newman Junior High School, Needham, Massachusetts; Paul Meunier, Marshfield High School, Marshfield, Massachusetts; Father Patrick Nowlan, O.S.A., Monsignor Bonner High School, Drexel Hill, Pennsylvania; Frank Oppenheimer, University of Colorado, Boulder, Colorado; Charles M. Shull, Jr., Colorado School of Mines, Golden Colorado; Malcolm K. Smith, Massachusetts Institute of Technology, Cambridge, Massachusetts; Moddie D. Taylor, Howard University, Washington, D.C.; Carol A. Wallbank, Dighton-Rehoboth Regional High School, Rehoboth, Massachusetts; Richard Whitney, Roxbury Latin School, West Roxbury, Massachusetts; Marvin Williams, Bell Junior High School, Golden, Colorado; M. Kent Wilson, Tufts University, Medford, Massachusetts; and Carl Worster, Belmont Junior High School, Lakewood, Colorado.

I also wish to acknowledge the invaluable services of George D. Cope and Joan E. Hamblin in photography; R. Paul Larkin as art director for the preliminary edition; Barbara Griffin, Nancy Nelson, and Gertrude Rogers in the organization of feedback from the pilot schools; Nathaniel C. Burwash and John W. DeRoy in apparatus construction and design; Benjamin T. Richards for production; and Andrea G. Julian for editorial assistance. Much of the administrative work was done by Geraldine Kline.

Throughout the entire project I benefited from the advice and criticism of M. Kent Wilson. Valuable assistance in coordinating various group efforts in the summers of 1963 and 1966 was provided by Byron L. Youtz. In editing this edition of the course, I was specially aided by Judson B. Cross and by Harold A. Pratt, who was responsible for the group summarizing the feedback.

I wish to thank the editorial and art staff of the Educational Book Division of Prentice-Hall, Inc., for their help in preparing the final form of this edition.

Constant sources of encouragement and constructive criticism were the pilot teachers, who voluntarily spent many extra hours relating to us their classroom experience. Without them, the course could not have been developed to this point.

The initial stage of the Introductory Physical Science Program was funded by Educational Services Incorporated. Since then, it has been supported by a grant from the National Science Foundation. This financial support is gratefully acknowledged.

Uri Haber-Schaim
March 1967

Index